The Breaking Process

Colin Winter

THE BREAKING PROCESS

SCM PRESS LTD

334 00139 0

First published 1981 by
SCM Press Ltd
58 Bloomsbury Street London WC1

Filmset by John Smith, London
and printed in Great Britain by
Richard Clay (The Chaucer Press) Ltd,
Bungay, Suffolk

*I dedicate this book
to Jane SLG
whose prayers and
understanding
have constantly supported me
in my own
breaking process*

Contents

Preface

This book existed before a word of it was ever written. The people whose lives have inspired it are still struggling, laughing, singing and dying in daily battles against cruel tyrants, exploitative systems, appalling governments. Their unyielding courage and their vision for a new world is behind what I have tried to say and why I wish to say it. Namibia's struggle is not the only one, though clearly it is the one to which I have committed my life. But humanity struggles throughout the world for the freedom to be free and the church is either standing with and supporting the oppressed, or she is sheltering behind, and therefore an accomplice of, the oppressor's violence. British society is again polarized between rich and poor. In Britain the workers, the struggling poor, the great masses of the unemployed are waiting for the church to identify with their struggle, to take up their cause, that of creating a new and juster society. It is high time the church came out from hiding behind the cloaks of the rich and the influential and took up a firm stand with the oppressed here. To do this she will have to undergo a breaking process herself. What this entails is the subject of this book.

1

Will the Real Church Please Stand Up?

I was born in a terrace house at 32 Balfour Street, Hanley, in a row of houses, two up two down, complete with outside pit lavatory at the bottom of a yard. That place put its seal on me for the rest of my life. It made me a non-belonger in what, I believe, is the most class-ridden nation in the world. From the very moment of birth, my destiny had been determined for me: I was one of the non-important people – i. e. non-public school, non-middle class, non whatever the in-thing was. Basically, I was non-rich, or put the other way, I was born poor.

The backyard step was my first contact with the outside world. From there I saw a world of working-class, poor people all around me. They were potters and miners, shop assistants and gypsies, shoe repairers and crate makers, coal merchants and bargees, there was a man who sold props for clothes lines and a purveyor of milk from a horse-drawn trap. There was also a whole army of unemployed. From that doorstep I had my first fights, saw my first bonfire night and experienced death for the first time when an ambulance carried away a youth who died from pneumonia. I was engulfed by a world of dirt, smoke and industrial pollution. It was a fight to keep clean and stay clean. From there I ventured out to learn to swim in the local canal and play football on a nearby rubbish tip.

I carry with me today vivid irreplaceable memories of a childhood in which I was surrounded by swearing, spitting, brawling, drunkenness, shouting, arguments, gang fights, humour, roguery, prostitution, wit, sporting characters like Stanley Matthews – these were my friends, real people, the kind of people whom I love and still admire to this day. I am proud to be one of them and know them to be my people. I feel one with them in their struggles, in their hopes, in their memories and attitudes. Having shared the same past, we share the same future. They take a lot of crushing. Their capacity for survival has always impressed me: but so has their inventiveness and humour. In our street there was a woman who loaned you 2s. 6d on a Monday and charged 6d interest rate on Friday – if you could make money in Balfour Street, you could make money anywhere! She also sold ginger beer on Sunday afternoons in a bottle with a marble for a stopper. I remember this because the contents of one bottle exploded over my jersey. At five, when you have spent your last tuppence on a disaster area, these memories are hard to erase.

There are other memories too. From that doorstep, I watched as four youths smashed up my 3-wheel bicycle – a Christmas present I was never to ride. I was four at the time. It goes without saying they had been given no presents that Christmas. From there I learnt my first words – swear words included, a vital part of an exploited people's vocabulary and very necessary at times to soothe their inner rage to shout at friend and foe alike. I learnt other words too – deadly words that struck terror into poor people's eyes, words like pneumonia, silicosis, TB, asthma, diptheria. And I picked up political words that brought looks of fear, anger or contempt into people's faces – like boss, stuck up, the queen, on the dole, out of work, posh, means test.

I saw other things too. From my mother I learnt how the poor share. 'Take this soup to Mrs Davidson, and don't tell anybody ...', ... bring that boy home for tea' (so she could wash him). And from my father, 'Where are my new brown shoes!' She, 'Gone.' He, 'Gone where!' She, 'Gone to Wales on the feet of an old miner, that's where.' End of dialogue.

From that back door step I met many fearlessly honest people, whom I shall call the struggling poor. Posturing was what they could not stand and would not take. When my father ventured his name as a Tory councillor for a 99.9% Labour ward, my brother conveyed to him the sundry messages of 'goodwill' from the numerous well-wishers, sons of miners and potters, at his primary school. The poster disappeared rapidly along with his day dreams of political privilege. Whenever I have seen prelates and priests parading with liturgical pomp in pageants, the brisk comment of an erstwhile eight-year-old companion, whose name and face have long since been forgotten, spring to mind. The first time we crept into church during a service, he whispered, 'Santa Claus'.

When the church dares face up to the devastating honesty of the poor, the breaking process has begun in earnest. Religious posturing is not on: workers respect an honest commitment to principles and admire dedication. Shams they see through and denounce.

Is all this important? Vitally, if I am to attempt a genuine theology. I have no illusions: very few of these great real people will read this. After all, why should they? I cannot blame them: they are not book people. And, anyway, they have been ignored by the church for so long that, like the song, they have learnt to get along without her very well.

The long historic attachment of the established church in this country to the wealthy, the powerful, the influential needs no re-counting by me. The vast majority of my kind of people still feel awkward, unwanted, unwelcome in it and would hardly wish to venture near it, except perhaps when forced to do so for a wedding or a funeral. They would deem it 'posh' with all that word means in terms of alienation, privilege and the pain of rejection. It certainly seems detached from their life. The vicar's house, for example, is usually the only detached one in a working-class area. If he originally came from the ranks of the workers, he has now probably joined the ranks of 'them', the bosses. His culture will most often have changed, for by training he will have been assimilated into the middle class, so even if he started by being working class – he will take *The Daily Telegraph* and send his kids to private schools. He will speak differently. He may even be kind, jolly (many are), a good bloke, but he has become one of 'them'. For my kind of people, the parson on those ads which say 'one lump or two' is their image of the local vicar, no matter how much the latter may protest.

The workers in Balfour Street had learnt to get on without the church very well. They had been doing it for centuries. They formed their own trades union, organized their own working men's club, visited their own sick and took care of each others problems. My childhood saw the days when they closed ranks against poverty and the probing eyes of the powerful. For those few workers who were 'religious' there was a tin hut called 'The Gospel Mission'. Here workers preached, prayed and sang gospel hymns to each other – a

3

minority of maybe twenty adults and a hundred children. It has gone now, inevitably swept away by the welfare state. The kids in the fifties, sixties and seventies did not need the annual bus trip to local beauty spots as we did, nor did the prospect of an annual prize giving or sports day keep them awake at nights, their blood tingling with excitement as ours did.

Yet today, the grandchildren of my childhood contemporaries will be facing the same dole queue that my forebears faced in the thirties. They already know the sense of frustration, hopelessness and anger that ate into the soul of my father's generation, the veterans of the post-1918 war. What has got to happen for the church to identify with the struggle of these young people today? What can possibly move it to relate to their needs and to share in the achievement of a society where unemployment will be regarded as a sin against humanity?

There are, of course, countries throughout the world where the church has taken the side of the poor. In Namibia, where my church is persecuted and hated, it has opted to make a clear stand with the poor and the oppressed. There are no poor in Britain,' I was told by a comfortable worshipper in a well-to-do congregation recently. The thought leapt into my mind that exactly the same sentence was used about South Africa by a cabinet minister there. Viewed from a palace, a stately home or from the rose lawns of suburbia, this statement is easy to make and many, here and there, believe it. But Christianity did not begin from the vantage point of the comfortably off. Jesus' first view of the world was that of a displaced person in a shanty: his last view was from the naked poverty of the cross. His option for the poor spans these two points in history. He was born poor, lived poor, died poor. If the church in Britain is to bear true witness to the gospel, if it is to discover its real ministry, it must find it in his. God loves poor people: that is both a scandal and an irritant to the rich. If God does, why are the poor so seldom seen in our churches and why do they feature so small in our concerns? I suppose it helps a lot if your starting point was the back doorstep of 32 Balfour Street, Hanley, but if it was not, then the New Testament asks you to see the world from where he saw it, in the stark poverty and rejection of the cowshed at Bethlehem. That is the beginning of the breaking process.

The church must break with its long association with the rich, with what we would be right to call its long historic past, if it is to be true to

4

its earliest traditions. There has to be a breaking process in which it is moved out of love and compassion to choose the side of the poor in our society. It must break with the rich, release itself from their control and their domination of its life and thinking. It is no good its pleading that it is neutral. In a class-divided society as unequal as ours is in Britain, such an argument is indefensible: neutrality in absolute terms is to opt for the powerful against the weak. But all this presupposes an understanding that we are a divided society in Britain and that poor and marginalized people exist here. But the church lumbers on as if this were not so or, if it is, that it does not matter. It then chooses options which are irrelevancies as far as ordinary people are concerned. This inevitably leads to a church which is judged itself to be an irrelevance.

Who are the poor in Britain? The answer to that question is as much political as it is theological. Put another way, the question of the poor in the church involves not only the God we believe in but the social conflict we live in. In the language of Gustavo Gutierrez, '... the poor today, rather than being regarded as a "problem for the Church", raise the question of what "being the Church" really means.'[1]

In Namibia it is clear what the church is about: it is a voice speaking out on behalf of and in defence of oppressed people. Society knows this. 'So you belong to a kaffir church,' a white businessman in Windhoek was asked by a colleague in a bar. The word used has heavy racist overtones and is used in contempt when whites speak in a derogatory fashion about blacks. The man's business associate was in no doubt that his friend's church stood on the side of the oppressed, though he was not too charmed by the fact. A second fact is also to be noted. As soon as this happens, the rich become uneasy, withdraw their support if their threats are not adhered to and, in the end, harass or persecute the church. The church hierarchy know this as if by instinct. By background and training they feel uneasy when this happens, keep quiet or seek to appease both sides. Where racial injustice or economic exploitation leads to violent confrontation between the contending parties, silence is no longer a plausible option. In this situation the church faces the breaking process: speak out and die, keep quiet and live.

In Namibia it became a political issue to care for poor people. There the poor were politics. They were mostly always black, and to respond to their plight was seen by whites as an automatic condemnation of the white system. Though it was clear to impartial outsiders that the apartheid system exploited and dehumanized blacks, whites saw nothing basically wrong with it. Jesus faced this situation frequently when he responded to the needs of poor people. The rich murmured against him, wanted to stone him or use other means of killing him. The sequence of events is nearly always the same: the first act of offering a cup of cold water in an oppressive society ultimately leads to the threat of violence. The Christian becomes exposed. The very existence of the poor must lead a Christian to examine the foundations of the society in which the 'have nots' exist and need his aid. In Namibia the breaking process went as follows:

1. The poor were visible everywhere: whites were visibly well fed, their private homes, schools, hospitals, old peoples homes were constructed out of the best material available and were lavishly furnished. The blacks lived in shanties or in the poorest quality housing available. Whites were visibly well off, well-dressed and healthy. They drove in cars. Blacks were mostly poor, ill-fed, and walked. One in two of their children in certain areas died before they were five. The black aged in Windhoek looked like Belsen victims.

2. When asked why this scandalous social difference existed, whites replied that blacks were used to nothing better. The majority of white Christians took this view too – some, a few, were concerned about it, a lesser few were deeply troubled.

3. For this last group, 'a minority within a minority', those who were unhappy about the economic and social gap, the gospel was a breaking process. It challenged the whole *status quo* and one's acquiesence in a violent exploitative society. It forced one to act, to speak out. Because the result of so doing led to threats, police harassment, persecution, very few did it. For those who did, deportation was inevitable. Thus three Anglican bishops have been deported from Namibia, all our white missionaries have been removed. Visas are not granted by the South African government when sought for doctors, nurses, teachers, priests, mechanics or others to work there.

What of Britain? Here a vast social and economic gulf divides our society, for those who will take the trouble to discover it, but, nevertheless, the rich/poor division which exists here is blurred. The press and TV rarely challenge the right of the rich to remain rich in the midst of the poverty of the poor. Nor does the church here take on the approach say of the early church fathers such as St Basil, St John Chrysostom or others. I am constantly being asked by rich people, Who are the poor in our society? What is the cause and what is the nature of their poverty? How poor are the poor here? Is their poverty inevitable, unavoidable or, given present world conditions, can anyone be blamed that poor exist? Is their poverty their own fault, is it self-imposed? Could they escape it by greater effort, stronger self-discipline, a more determined effort? If a Prime Minister rose from being a shop girl in a small provincial town to high office, cannot others make it, given the same effort and determination to succeed?

In Namibia the poor challenged the church out of our smugness and our sunny disposition to make things appear better than they were. The poor came to us for food for starving children, for money to pay fines imposed by an apartheid regime. Their lives were broken by hundreds of government laws which daily yoked them to a state of subservience and wretchedness. We entered that same breaking process in so far as we were prepared to stand with them in their struggle for a more just and humane society. To be a Christian in that society necessitated believing in God and being prepared to enter into social conflict. The whole violence of the State was ready to be unleashed against any who were prepared to question even the smallest injustice or call in question even the slightest piece of unjust legislation. In this process the poor themselves have divided the church. They are God's two-edged sword, cutting through the hypocrisy, the cant and the evasiveness that passes for Christian behaviour in an apartheid society. The dividing line comes between those who will opt for justice and those who defend an unjust system; between those who, through their contact and love for the oppressed, see the evil of a system which denies them the right to be human and those who do not. One begins with the offer of a cup of cold water and ends with the possibility of being put on trial for treason. The poor have not only challenged our Christianity by the just demands they make on us, but they also have challenged the political system which crushes them. The church is then forced to examine, in the light of the gospel, the whole realm of policies which is responsible for their miserable estate.

The whole process leads to the critical examination of everything the church says or does in the light of its significance for the oppressed themselves. They become our judges. Thus, when, for example, in South Africa a bishop makes a statement about human rights, this can be heralded in the West as courageous and outspoken, given the present South African government's reputation for clamping down on its opponents. The bishop may feel he has satisfied both the demands of his conscience and of the gospel. But when the same statement is taken up by the oppressed themselves, examined and discussed, in the majority of instances it is rejected as being weak, irrelevant and too little too late. Instead of the church being the sign of the kingdom, a message of hope, a light set on a hill, it becomes an escape route for white consciences. The church, in order to understand itself, has looked inwards on itself and has a comfortable feeling that, in relation to its past, it has become fairly radical, rather progressive. In a situation where the poor have become our teachers, the church has to do its thinking not from above, where bishops or a powerful elite dominate its life and control its actions, but from beneath where the poor are really being listened to and their counsels are being reflected in the church's praxis. In such a situation the breaking point has been reached and past: 'being born as a church means dying to a history of oppression and complicity'. There is a dying process demanded here: the poor will either reject the church and turn away from it to where they can work for their own liberation, or they will liberate it by being allowed to speak to it and, through it, to their oppressors within it and in the outside world. In Namibia this process has taken place and is continuing to lead the church into head-on collision with an alien and violent state. The process has been a costly one as far as the church itself is concerned, but it is one which has given it a new life and vigour. Furthermore, it is able to draw immense strength from the experience of a New Testament which speaks to it about a similar situation which faced the early church. Scripture, which the church needs to inspire it, to guide it and to give it strength, speaks to us in a way which has often been lost or obscured for the Western Christian.

X, a Christian minister was taken for questioning in Namibia by the Special Branch. Thrown into a cell for no obvious reason, he was deprived of his freedom. He felt an inner violence towards God. Frightened at the prospect of torture or prolonged arrest, he flung away from him a Bible which had been given him as his sole reading material. His anger blazed against God who had tolerated the daily suffering of the oppressed Namibian people for over one hundred years. He did not wish to read the Bible, let alone pray. After a while, in the loneliness of the prison cell, he felt a prolonged calm. He felt no more fear, no more anger. Calmly he walked over to where he had flung the Bible, opened its pages and felt a peace such as he had never experienced in his life before. Later that day he told a confused police interrogator he was ready to die and that they could kill him immediately if they wished to. They had no longer any power over him. Within a week they released him. As he left he challenged his tormentors. 'I haven't finished with you yet,' he told a startled captain of police, 'so you can't release me. I have a responsibility to God for your soul.' The breaking process had been met, conquered and a new man emerged. This is not a single once-and-for-all event, but a process that will have to be dealt with day in, day out as that pastor struggles each day with the evils of an apartheid regime. What was the gospel for him at that moment? I suppose he would say it was that which enabled him to conquer his fear.

The gospel breaks us. This is the clear fact that emerges. It challenges our comfortable lives, our cosy theories and our carefully planned futures. Like the Syro-Phoenician woman, the poor hammer on our doors, will not shut up and refuse to go away.

The gospel was delivered to the church to be preached throughout the world. The tragedy in Britain is, what do the poor do when they cannot see this happening, when they challenge the very church that is supposed to be preaching it and denounce it because of the way the church conducts its affairs, ignores the cries of the oppressed or is actually engaged in their oppression? In such cases does the church, like Israel of old, forfeit the right to be called the church? Does God replace it with something more worthy of his requirements? Do the poor form a para-church which will instinctively serve their needs more effectively than the one which excludes them? Is there one church for the rich and another for the poor and, if so, is the former an idolatrous church which simulates worship but is in reality a bogus shambles which worships the Nothings, to use the psalmist's words for the idols of this world? If a church fails to proclaim and to live out the gospel, are the poor supposed to wait forever, for a long while, or just a little while until it reforms itself and welcomes them in? If the poor are not welcomed into the church, can it not be said that Jesus is excluded also? If Jesus is excluded in the person of the poor, what hope is there for that church? When ordinary people, and they exist in their thousands in Britain today, turn away from organized religion in despair, for some of the reasons mentioned above, what is to become of them? Who is to pastor them? Has God abandoned them? Must they remain secular Christians, knowing in their conscience they cannot sit through meaningless liturgies, listening to platitudes for sermons as mute members of a church which does not face the real problems facing ordinary people, let alone attempts dialogue with those engaged in the agonies that face us in the last part of this century?

Are we, in fact, a special case in Britain and Western Europe? At first sight, on reading the following statement by Gutierrez, we seem to be. He can write the following of the poor of the Third World, but would we write it, say, of Britain or the rest of Western Europe?

> Great efforts have been made to blot out the memory of the oppressed. This deprives them of a source of energy, historical will and rebellion. Their memory still lives on in cultural expressions, popular religion, and the resistance to impositions by the church bureaucracy. The memory of Christ is present in every hungry, thirsty, oppressed and humiliated person, in the despised races and the exploited classes, this memory of Christ who for freedom has set us free. (Gal. 5.1)[2]

Is the memory of Christ present in the two million unemployed workers in this country? Is his memory present in the 150,000 homeless men in the city of London and in the great sprawling cities of Western Europe where the unemployed are dumped and then abandoned by the rest of society to rot and disintegrate, marginalized at the fringes of our society? Certainly the memory of Jesus can be readily seen in the repeated acts of helpfulness, caring, sharing and genuine compassionate concern that the 'dossers' in my part of London show to each other day after day. But is the memory of Christ present in the majority of those churches that count such people as nuisance value, accept the policies of governments that regularly

10

tolerate the continuing presence of the unemployed in our midst and show a cruel indifference to their continuing existence?

For a church to be reborn in Britain today, is it not essential that it must give a clear option, not a mere tokenism, to the poor and oppressed in our midst? Would not this option drive it to a passionate crusade on the part of the unemployed, the homeless, the black community, the weak and the unhoused? Would it not necessitate the giving up of the privileges that still today clutter the church and prevent it from making a clear stand with the poor? How can a rich church understand, comfort, uphold or even acknowledge the existence of the poor in her midst when she is so clothed in the defiled garments of class, wealth and privilege? Does not such a church have to turn its own history upside down in order to come into line with the freedom song by which the virgin Mary sings out God's praise? 'He has put down the mighty from their seat and has exalted the humble and meek.' If such sentiments, which were the hallmark of the early church, are to be more than musical canticles sung in near-empty cathedrals, should not the church, which has been commissioned by Jesus to proclaim that gospel from the house-tops, start proclaiming it in the street and alley ways of our land? The established church reflects the established state in teaching us that law and order of itself is something intrinsically good. But this is too superficial: law which favours the rich and ignores the just complaints of the poor, which holds down the workers (who still compose the greatest part of our society) and favours the rich, has to be judged in the light of the same scripture. If the gospel as defined in Luke 4 is a liberation process, then clearly it has something great and important to say to the workers, to those shut out from the decision-making of the powerful and to the nobodies of our society. The gospel message uproots all injustice and establishes friendship and love.

We live in a society in which confrontation is a daily experience. My experiences in Namibia led me to believe that when the church there stood with the poor, the exploited workers, the weak and those condemned to an endless life of poverty, that we were then siding with those who were specially near and dear to God. I have had the same experience when standing with weak or marginalized people here. The church is reluctant here to take sides, or rather it has already taken sides. It tacitly stands with the rich, the powerful and the

11

influential in our society. In its leanings and disposition it is seen by the poor to be for the rich, no matter how much it may claim impartiality.

There are Christians who will respond by saying they are as much against the power of the unions as they are against the greed of the capitalists. Whereas I believe the trade union movement can be reformed, I do not believe the basic principles of capitalism can. It is based first and last on the profit motive at all cost, is a killer as far as the Third World is concerned and must be replaced by a more just and fairer system.

But there is a main point I wish to emphasize and it concerns the gospel. I believe one of my tasks in Britain today is to free the church from domination by the rich and restore it again to the poor who have been systematically excluded from it certainly from the time of the industrial revolution onwards. This may seem a brash and offensive statement, but I mean it. I believe if this could be achieved we would see the emergence of a truly people's church which by its very nature would attract those who today have fled from the church as it is presently constituted or who ignore it from disgust or because they feel it is plainly irrelevant. I believe a church so composed would bring back again to Britain some of the freshness and loving concern shown in the Acts of the Apostles. Jesus said the sign of the kingdom was that the poor have the gospel preached to them. The church of which I speak would honour the workers and share with them the vision of the kingdom. First, it would listen to them and take up their cause. It could then speak to them the mighty themes of the gospel, seeing them as co-creators in God's universe. In so doing it would accord them a dignity which capitalism has stripped from them. It would recapture with them the vision of a just and caring society. Such a church would begin by doing penance for its own complicity in the exploitation of the poor. For the sake of the poor it would learn to give away its lands, its possessions and live liberated from its obsessive clinging to material wealth and the patronage of the rich. It would become again a serving church which humbly and with deep love serves the poorest as did its Lord. It would not hate the affluent or the mighty, but would show them that man does not live by bread alone and liberate them from their addiction to wealth by freeing them to be loved by the poor.

12

In my love for the poor, am I leaving myself open to the charge that I am being excessively sentimental about them? After all, there are kind, nice and good rich people. We know dozens who are. Am I not guilty then of speaking of the poor as a special case and in danger of making them always the goodies and the rich the baddies? Is not this an absurdity, something which militates against logic and is plainly untrue? After all, the poor are just as capable of murder, cheating, lying, swindling, violence, as the rich, so why treat them as though they are a special case? The simple answer is because God does! This is the clear biblical message from the beginning. Because the poor are the victims of injustice, God in Jesus has made them a special case: He has opted for them. The poor will inherit the kingdom.

In the Bible, poverty is not in itself something to be applauded. It is in fact a wretched condition. Rich Christians romanticize it, misinterpreting the text 'blessed are the poor in spirit', as when they claim, 'I wish I were poor. Their lives are uncomplicated, more simple. The poor don't have the worries of the rich.' Poverty is not an ideal state. On the contrary, it is regarded as an evil condition in the Bible, because the poor are victims of injustice and oppression. Poverty is seen not so much as an absence of possessions but as a condition of powerlessness. So poverty is not an ideal but an evil.

In the Old Testament various words are used to describe the poor. Today poverty usually means an absence of money, or possessions. Hebrew too speaks of this kind of poverty as an absence of things, but the main emphasis is on dependency, powerlessness or weakness. The Old Testament stresses the poor as victims of oppression and injustice.

Jesus said he was fulfilling in his person the hopes of the poor. 'He has sent me to bring good news to the poor ... to proclaim the Lord's year of favour' (Luke 4.18). He had come to take up the cause of the weak, the helpless, those whom society rips off. This was clearly his option: is it ours? The poor were his priority: where do they stand in our list of priorities? In fact who are the powerless ones among us? The following list immediately occurs to me. They are the thousands of workers just dumped on to the dole through government closure of their factories and places of work and totally helpless to do anything about it. They are the young couples living in one room flats with parents or in appalling damp-ridden housing. They are homeless men and women living in poor-quality hostels or roaming the streets, the flotsam and jetsam of our cities. They are youngsters on housing estates unable to find jobs, hating themselves and drifting into violence. They are victims of police violence. They are battered wives and women assaulted or degraded by their male partners and trapped into submission through lack of an alternative place to live or to go. They are black youth, harassed by society, discriminated against in schools and unable to find jobs and, along with white youth, the victims of policies that aim to bring down inflation through increasing unemployment. They are refugees who arrive from areas of war, famine, or political persecution and are dumped uncaringly in our major cities to fend for themselves. They are immigrants who are terrorized by such groups as the National Front.

And what does it mean to love these helpless, marginalized people? The church is good at bringing them words of comfort, offering a sandwich here, a cup of tea there, but this does not get to grips with the causes which lie behind their suffering; it does not deal with the injustice that has made them helpless. The good news Jesus brought was that God himself had taken up their cause. The Christ had come as their liberator. The poor are not seeking palliatives, nor do they want sympathy. What they need is what Jesus offered – freedom. But can the poor be liberated from above? Again Jesus' example is a telling one: 'the word was made flesh and dwelt among us'. He was among them, one with them, bone of their bone, flesh of their flesh. He opted to be totally at one with them in solidarity with their sufferings and struggles.

So the gospel begins with the affirmation of an emptying process. Jesus stripped himself of power to be born poor. This divine self-emptying is the very source and inspiration of the gospel message (Phil. 2.6-8). That which Jesus effected can no longer be considered a counsel of perfection for his church. If the world is to take us seriously, we must go and do likewise. Yet there is a manifest joy awaiting those who, inspired by the Spirit, can make this option for the poor their own reality. Such a church has been beautifully described by Santa Ana in *Towards a Church of the Poor*:

> We are aware of the price that must be paid to give concrete shape to this church of the poor. That awareness comes from the actual

experience of brothers and sisters who are fully committed to this undertaking. They form confessing communities, perpetually on the move: today consoling the victims of oppression and torture; tomorrow perhaps confronting economic powers that do not pay the workers proper wages; the day after, very possibly struggling for the rights of the peasants, who are often forced to emigrate because the mechanisms that permit the application of the laws of the market appear to condemn them to poverty. This church, the church of the poor, is no longer a prop for the interests of the powerful. With Hannah and Mary it sings that the Lord is to put down the mighty from their thrones and exalt those of low degree, filling the hungry with good things and sending the rich empty away (cf. I Sam. 2.1-10; Luke 1.47-55). It is not a case of a church that hates the powerful and the rich; the Church of Jesus Christ cannot hate any human being.

It is to this Church, then, that we invite you. We invite you to the living experience of giving priority to the poor, not only in pro-grammes of service but in actual evangelization, to learn from them, to travel with them, to draw up church programmes and projects from their side of history, which means doing so *with* them, so that they are really *their* projects and programmes, not simply *for* them. This church is the Church of Christ, to whom we all desire to be faithful. The experience of our brothers and sisters is that the poor find in that Church the presence of him who was called Emmanuel: God with us.[3]

Its opposite, I suppose, is that which most tourists see as they pile out of their coaches and are charged their thirty or sixty pence to be taken on a guided tour of those cathedrals that charge visitors for the privilege of entering them. I am unmoved by the arguments of those who see this as the only way of maintaining these shrines. I would much prefer the upkeep of them to be the responsibility of the state, a national heritage that evokes national pride and a national budget to support them as is the case in Sweden and other Scandinavian countries. Commercialism enhances neither the church nor its teaching.

STRIKE ACTION

It was rotten of you,
Lord, to curse that fig tree.
I mean, what had it done
to deserve it?
Nothing.
I can't excuse you,
because it wasn't even
the time of figs, so how
could you expect to
find fruit on it?
Please be reasonable:
you can hardly blame people
for saying you were mad,
if you went around the place
doing things like that.
May I take a minute or so
of your time to remind you
what happened?
I clear my throat –
You had come to Bethany
and felt hungry, so you
went out to see if there
were any figs on this tree.
But it wasn't the time
to gather fruit. (Now, being
you, you must have known
that.) Then, according to all
the evidence, you just
blasted it. You must have
done because it withered.
I just don't get it.

Is the answer found in what
happened next?
You went to Jerusalem,
entered the Temple,
looked around
and as it was already
late you went to Bethany
with the twelve.
Next day you came back,
entered the Temple and drove
out the racketeers.
The Pharisees went mad when they
heard what you'd done in
there, flinging over the
tables, and hurling out
all those big business
tycoons.
But the poor people
went mad with delight –
a different kind of
madness, I agree.
Then Peter drew your attention
to that poor dead tree.
It's withered away, rabbi,
he said, confused as we.
Another clue
was this quotation
which comes to mind,
Whoever keeps a fig
tree expects to eat of
its fruits.

16

But not the fruits of robbery
with violence, not
ripping off the poor,
not all those
dirty deals and shady
practices that had taken
root inside your Father's house –
that is until you threw them out.
God just can't stand oppressors.
Remember how he had blasted the
Egyptians, spread fire
across their land,
smote their vines and
fig trees before he led
the people out of bondage?
The Egyptians were
glad to see the back of
them – I bet!
Lord, I think I get
it now.
You came to that temple as
liberator, like your Father
before you, expecting to
find fruits of justice
and fair dealing. You found
only the stench of cooking
meat and cooked books.
You had to smite the
fig tree to show that
you can't stand a church
that turns religion into
big business.
But the cash
registers are back in
our cathedrals, Lord.
Your church is run by
bankers trained in the
city. Will you have to
smite us again, as you did
that fig tree, before we
bring forth the fruits
of righteous dealing?

2

The Gospel as Solidarity with the Poor

In 1972, a few weeks after being deported from Namibia by the South African government, I made a lonely pilgrimage to the United Nations in New York, the place to which the powerless in Namibia look for protection but so far look in vain. I wanted to add my voice to those of others who over the years since 1948 have spoken there on the Namibian issue. I was determined to make known to the world powers represented there just what South Africa was doing to the poor people of Namibia. My message was simple: people were dying there. I hoped to convince the United Nations that it was time for action and that there was a limit to what a captive people could endure. I had my say, was listened to with respect and then came out of the chamber. Later my speech came out as yet one of thousands which have consumed tons of paper that has piled up in the UN over the issue of Namibia.

As I made to leave the building, I was stopped by some of the SWAPO representatives who asked me to join them in a nearby room. They had asked me specially to say some prayers with them. These men explained they had been away from home, some for thirteen, fourteen or fifteen years, and when I looked over the group, all heads were bowed in intensive prayer. You cannot falsify such moments. Though heart-broken at being forced to leave Namibia, yet with these fellow exiles I felt totally at one. Solidarity is the only word to describe it.

In 1980 I was invited to attend the independence celebrations of the newly liberated Zimbabwe. During the week's festivities I visited the home of one of the leaders of the revolution. I spent a couple of hours meeting and talking to freedom fighters and again on leaving I was asked to pray. I was shown into a room which was packed with people who had fought in the bush for their country's independence. Again there was the same intense feeling of reverence and awe in the presence of God, which those who know Africa intimately will understand. I relate these two incidents – two among many – to indicate my anger at Western Christians who condemn those engaged in the liberation struggle as though they were mindless killers. In Belfast recently I spent two hours in a church meeting answering question after question about Africans who have taken up arms to liberate their country. My reports of the appalling atrocities under which black people suffered and struggled in Namibia, South Africa and Rhodesia were either ignored or regarded as irrelevant and swept aside by my hosts who launched attack after attack on the violence used by the oppressed to liberate themselves. They were far more concerned about what might happen to whites and cared nothing about what was actually happening to blacks. Never once did they condemn or even mention the violence of the white oppressors. It was only after I had returned to London that I was informed that my hosts, who were all middle-class white members of the Presbyterian church, belong to a church which is unique in Christendom: it is the only one which has in its charter the right to defend its constitution by force of arms! Yet this church, along with some others in Western Europe, wages a constant battle against the World Council of Churches' Programme to Combat Racism. It is highly significant that those churches which have made the loudest protest against the grants given by the Programme to Combat Racism are largely rich, white and Western.

But there is a further reason which so far has been fairly obscured in the West. There is a fully planned and directed crusade directed by the South African Department of Information aimed at totally discrediting the World Council of Churches, particularly the Programme to Combat Racism, which uses extreme right-wing political movements and religious sects in Britain and elsewhere. Once opposed to each other, these groups are now combining to denounce the spread of Marxism and the terrorist threat to South Africa. Such groups as the extreme right-wing Christian League of Southern Africa, having fled from its headquarters in Salisbury, Zimbabwe, after the victory of the Patriotic Front, announced that it would continue the struggle from South Africa. Derrick Knight, in his latest book *Beyond the Pale*,[1] has exposed the activities of the individuals who run them on behalf of South Africa. Their pronouncements are picked up regularly by the right-wing press in Britain and from such reports, which are always slanted in South Africa's favour, the racism which exists in so many white churches here is fanned and kept alive.

This is not to say that the poor and oppressed themselves are without their own spokesmen: though these are rarely allowed a voice in the Western press, they do exist and at such meetings as the Nairobi conference and the PCR meeting in Amsterdam, they are eloquent and effective speakers. What I find exciting and personally strengthening is that the poor and the oppressed of the world are now producing their own spokesmen both in politics and in religion. If the rich churches in the West have been the worst critics of the World Council of Churches' Programme to Combat Racism, it is also significant to note that the poor churches themselves have been overwhelmingly supportive of its programme. So have the poor churches anything to teach the rich churches or, put more strongly, does God have anything to teach us through the words of the oppressed? What happens when the poor become our teachers? Well first, I suppose, they cut through our hypocrisy. They challenge us on our newly acquired pacifist stance. They ask us direct questions such as: Did your church condemn outright the American war in Vietnam? If you were silent in the face of this war of genocide, why single us out? Did you fight against the Nazis and their racist practices and unbridled violence? Why have the Christians in Germany, who were usually so silent during the regime of Hitler, become so strident now against our retaliation against violence? Does your church condemn the wholesale production of mass weapons of slaughter? Has it said or done anything to try and curb the mad escalation of the arms trade? Would you condemn church members in your own country who make fortunes out of producing arms or who work in factories which produce poison gas or napalm? They know our answers before we reply and their faces register their reaction. Christians in the West stand overwhelmingly silent when facing their own national arms proliferation, yet see no anomaly in judging the oppressed who resist their oppressors. A massacre took place in Cassinga in Southern Angola on Ascension Day, 1978. South African jets with high explosives bombed, strafed and then returned to drop phosphorous bombs against a SWAPO camp composed largely of Namibian students. After the assaults by the bombers, parachute troops dropped from aircraft and bayonetted women and children. The ultimate death toll was a thousand dead young people, the cream of Namibia's youth. The soldiers were quoted in the South African press later as saying, 'It was hell to have to shoot at women.'[2] There was hidden Western complicity in this appalling atrocity. An examination of the equipment used by the South African forces against the defenceless Namibian students, women and children revealed the following: the guns used were Belgian FLN rifles; the planes used were French Mirage jets; the transport planes were American manufactured; the Land Rovers were produced by a British Leyland subsidiary in South Africa. No one can prove that any or all of these articles of warfare were sold directly by these Western powers, but such niceties do not impress the relatives of the thousand slain. The point needs stressing that most Western countries are engaged in armaments manufacture on an enormous scale which is rarely ever challenged by the Christian churches in their own lands. Is it not time that we started to name the 'terrorists' in our ranks – those who make fortunes out of the sale of arms; those who invest in the arms trade and live in comfort off their stocks and shares, as well as those who invest in South African companies from whose taxes the South African government is enabled to wage war? These are not the major issues for the majority of churches in the West, but if the Western church could be roused to wage a moral crusade against investing in apartheid, I believe the consequences could be enormous but, until it does, is it any wonder that blacks in Southern Africa tell Christians in the West to cast out first the beam in our own eye before we attempt to remove the mote that is in theirs?

I was waiting to address an ecumenical conference in Toronto some years ago and happened to examine the books of recent theology which were on the well-equipped bookstall. As I was to speak on some of the problems facing the Third World, I glanced through the index of the works of a dozen or so leading Western theologians which were on show. None of them had in their indices a single mention of the word 'poor' or 'poverty'. I looked in vain for any reference to the world's poor. I felt that their works excluded the day-to-day living experience of two-thirds of humanity. Here was a classic example of the rich speaking to the rich about the problems of the rich. Is this what we have reduced Christianity to in the West? Where is the antidote to be found for this sickness? It is to be found in the spokesmen of the poor themselves.

During the past ten years I have crossed America annually on speaking and preaching trips. I know something of her people and her problems. I have met various political and spiritual leaders, but none impresses me more than James Cone. I see Cone in the role of liberator, not only for black Americans but also for white middle-class Americans too. Just as the God of the Bible raised up spokesmen from the very ranks of the oppressed themselves, so I believe he does the same through the witness, the writing and speaking of such men as James Cone. The breaking process seems to me eminently to be at work in him. In his book, *The God of the Oppressed*, he tells of his birth in Arkansas in a small town called Bearden. Two things there shaped his consciousness: 'the black Church experience and the socio-political significance of white people'.[3] The church gave him an irrepressible desire for freedom. From his experience in the black congregation in that tiny Arkansas town, Cone developed his understanding of Black Theology which for him is summarized as follows: 'to know Jesus is to know him as revealed in the struggle of the oppressed for freedom. Their struggle is Jesus' struggle, and he is thus revealed in the particularity of their cultural history – their hopes and dreams of freedom.'[4]

Cone has broken with the white understanding of God which he vehemently rejects. He writes: 'Whites devised various philosophical arguments for God's existence: blacks knew him as the God of history who liberated his people from oppression.'[5] But he is also the God who calls the poor and the weak to a newly-created existence. For black people Jesus means freedom. Because of his experience within this church and because he is black, Cone challenges the theorizing of most Western theologians. Their theology does not speak to his needs or answer his and his people's sufferings as black people. So he writes of white theologians: '... they seldom seem to get to the point that makes the Gospel the Gospel ... I want to know how reconciliation is related to Asia, Africa, Latin America and every other section of this human globe where people are oppressed socially, politically and

23

economically ... What are we to make of this doctrine where black people define the promised land as liberation from white oppression.'[6] What indeed!

Cone knows from a lifetime's experience the reaction of rich white Christians to his message and the dismissive attitudes of white theologians to what he has to say. His final remarks in his last chapter deserve to be quoted:

> Black theologians are not called to interpret the Gospel in a form acceptable to white oppressors. Our calling is derived from the people who have been through the trials and tribulations of this world. Our task is to interpret their struggle in the light of God's presence with them, liberating and reconciling the oppressed with himself. We must let white oppressors know that we are on the battle field of the Lord and we are determined through God's grace to fight until we die.[7]

This is hardly the style or manner in which most Western theologians write today, nor is it the material which finds its way into the majority of our popular works of devotion. The black theologian assumes the mantle of the prophet and challenges our racism – acknowledged or hidden – our affluence, in fact, what we stand for. More than this he feels the rage of the oppressed because he is still a part of them. Their pain is his pain: their humiliation his. This is how he differs from most Western theologians – he is himself oppressed.

In a different context, that of Latin America, Juan Luis Segundo quotes a Brazilian writer who stresses the vital importance of the theologian being at one with struggling people. He writes as follows: 'The function of the theologian is to systematize the critical reflection which the people makes of its practice in the light of faith. The theologian helps the people discover the liberative dimension of their faith.'[8]

Frei Betto, the writer Segundo is quoting, goes on to state that such a theological perception will enable the people to see God's designs in the day-to-day events of real life. The theologian is inseparably linked to the pastor. It is through his pastoral contact with real people that he is forced to deal with real issues. The people are not just passive observers of his activity but contribute to his theological thinking as

24

well. He draws on the powerful elements latent in the faith of the people. In this process the poor become our teachers.

But what are the poor seeking? Is there in the gospel itself something which is especially attractive to the poor and to which they can respond? Are not today's poor, the powerless, referred to in that statement of Jesus which says, 'Bless you, Father ... for hiding these things from the learned and the clever and revealing them to mere children ... for that is what it pleased you to do' (Matt. 11.25). There is something in the gospel that the poor can see which the powerful cannot see, namely that God has destined them for freedom. James Cone speaks for black Americans but he also speaks for the struggling poor everywhere: 'God's reconciliation means destroying all forms of slavery and oppression in white America so that the people of colour can affirm the authenticity of their political freedom.'[9] What theologians speak for the oppressed in Britain today?

In the Namibia Peace Centre which I have in the East End of London, some black students sent to us by the government of Zimbabwe were singing freedom songs about their struggle. These songs were mostly in their own language, but a few were in English. During the course of the evening, a homeless worker from Cardiff came to the Centre to see if we could help find him accommodation. He had never been in the house before and sat a little nervous at first, awkward in what were strange surroundings. After listening for an hour he quietly left. Next day he came round with a bunch of flowers and said how much the previous evening had meant to him. 'Their songs made me cry,' he said. Songs about the oppressed struggling for freedom against injustice had got through to him. Freedom is communicable to the struggling poor across racial and language boundaries.

How do the poor look at the gospel and what insights do they derive from it which they can share with us? I would like to draw my examples from Africa, Nicaragua and Czechoslovakia.

Dipheko is a black South African freedom fighter. His whole life has been one of struggle. He was thrown out of school at sixteen for shouting out during a school assembly 'Whose next?' when he heard of the death of prime minister Strijdom. From boyhood Jesus for him was the representative of the poor. He was easily attracted to Christianity because of its teaching of love for one's neighbour and doing unto others as you would they should do unto you – both especially

25

attractive to African society. He was repulsed from Christianity by the hypocritical attitude of church leaders in South Africa. Though he felt honoured when white priests came to his school and actually talked to him, this feeling soon waned when he realized that the black employees of those same white clergy were given dog meat to eat when they worked for these men in their white segregated homes. Where was all this 'do unto others' stuff he had heard so heartily commended in the school services? Church leaders were supposed to be custodians of the faith but were totally silent in the midst of torture, beatings, imprisonment of blacks, he said. Is Christianity serious? he asked himself.

He took his questions further and read Basil Davidson's book *Black Mother*, in which he learnt that when black slaves were being embarked on ships from the port of Luanda in Angola to America, Christian priests were brought in to baptize them before they set forth. They could not be sent abroad as 'barbarians'. He saw the church's role as a precursor of colonialism. 'Whereas there were individual Christians like George Moffat who had opened up 'the dark continent' and had brought schools and clinics, I could also see that after the Bible came the soldiers who took away the lands of the people. Though blacks had fought on the side of the whites in two major world wars, and in the first against Germany six hundred black soldiers had been killed in a ship called *The Mandy*, no credit was given them for this. It was all forgotten. I became a reluctant agnostic, asking myself, must I reject God because of the failure of the institution?' Stronger questions followed. The basic one which caused him most trouble was if God exists, what is he doing? 'He should be a very loving father, loving all his children. He should be concerned how his children are living,' he told me. Experience in South Africa had shown him otherwise.

For taking part in a planned revolution in South Africa he was sentenced to fifteen years in prison, three of which were spent in solitary confinement. During this time his only reading materials were two Bibles, one in English and one in Xosa, and various works on the Bible, which were obtainable from the prison library on Robben Island. He told me he had been able to read the Bible from cover to cover twice and was stimulated by it. He had read Koestler's book called *The Iron Cross* which treated Jesus as a figure in history, so he had no difficulty in believing in his actual existence. He found himself attempting to see Jesus in his own era as an ordinary man, looking at him in a role as reformer, trying to reform a corrupt society. 'I tried to look at him from a socialist point of view and as a dedicated revolutionary.' He noticed that Jesus had a different approach from the Zealots in trying for change by peaceful means, rallying not only Jews but appealing to Romans also. 'Now, put into my situation, though I recognized his revolutionary and political role, I disagreed with his tactics. Otherwise my own interpretation of him was that he was a very great man. I see him as a social reformer, deeply concerned about the social conditions under which the poor existed. I see him too as a victim of those who own the means of livelihood. They were the ones who ultimately succeeded in destroying him. Whereas I could never see Jesus as God, yet for me personally there was no doubt that he was a revolutionary – anyone who brings about a change, though not necessarily through violent means, new institutions from an old one, a new way of life altogether, is a revolutionary for me. Jesus' ultimate object was the bringing about of a new society.' This was the appeal Jesus had for an African freedom fighter.

He was released from solitary confinement in 1973 and formed a discussion group within the prison to discuss the revolutionary aspects of Jesus' teaching. Each person in the group was asked to take up a particular aspect, read up on it and then present it the following weekend to the rest. One day they asked a visiting white chaplain if Jesus was truly a revolutionary. The minister was terrified by their question. He told them that Jesus was the son of God who had come to find a place for them in heaven. He also promised he would bring back some books with him the following week to prove his point. He never in fact did come back! His final word to them had been 'That is a political discussion and a Christian should not be involved in politics.'

After his first trial the accused were all acquitted by a Jewish judge, but were immediately re-arrested and told by the police that they would be tried again. 'We'll get one of our own judges.' The judge who eventually tried them condemned them after a further hearing of four days. The Special Branch detective who was looking after him told him directly, 'You'll get fifteen years.' This is exactly what he did get.

27

When sentenced all the accused sang freedom songs and shouted slogans. 'We never thought we would serve the sentences. The OAU was vociferous. Algeria at that time was led by Ben Bella and Nkrumah and Nasser were shouting about marching through the streets of Johannesburg. So whilst our parents and the crowds were crying, we were laughing and shouting slogans.'

Did all this crush him? Far from it: though today recovering from the ravages of TB and stomach ulcers, he struggles on convinced in the ultimate invincibility of his cause, his people's freedom. I thought of him when I read a letter from Latin America in the WCC's *International Review of Mission*:

However it is not for lack of hope that we are telling these truths that sound like falsehoods but are realities, the products of the system of dependence and domination which western capitalism has imposed on us. Our soul is full of hope. We believe in life because we have seen death so often. We are wildly in love with that maize patch of the peasant who is tortured by the wandering military police, harassed and murdered by estate guards in Chisec, Ixcan, on the south coast, in the east, the north and the centre of the country, because that dead field blossoms and always will blossom with small communities alongside the maize fields, on the winding paths, by the brooks, in the little allotments, even in the small-holdings of this or that urban group.

Yes, indeed, for while the two words 'human rights' lose all meaning in the mouths of the great, the diplomats, the Kissingers, they assume a greater and greater wealth of meaning in the hearts of the little people, the weak, those who are endlessly exploited and despised. For in our constant dialogue with them, Jesus Christ is disclosing to us the magical secrets of life, in the light of the Word and of the struggle for a change of heart, a metanoia, in man and society. And in the helplessness and weakness of a community of simple people, persecuted, punished, we have glimpsed the strength of the Virgin Mary, the Baptist, Simeon ... For, despite everything, on the thin pale lips of hungry children a smile still lights up and transforms our grief into boundless hope.[10]

For me Dipheko is a living embodiment of hope. He never gave in to the apartheid system. He went into prison a 'D' class prisoner and came out after fifteen years in the same category. For fifteen years he starved. Does what Luke wrote (Luke 4.18-19) show us now that the liberation of the victims of economic and racial oppression is at the very heart of the gospel? The poor show us the real meaning of hope: it is the invincible courage to struggle on. The oppressed do not have to accept humiliation and suffering in this world: they are determined to change it.

For my second example I go to Latin America. It was Camilo Torres, the revolutionary priest, who said: 'I discovered Christianity as a life centred totally on love of neighbour. It was later that I discovered in Colombia you cannot bring about this love simply by beneficence. There were needed a whole change of political, economic and social structures. These changes demanded revolution. That love was intimately bound up with revolution.'[11] He was killed at Carmen, Colombia, on 15 April 1961. His death fulfilled his statement: 'I am a revolutionary because I am a priest.' His identification with the struggling poor caused him to be reduced to lay status by the Cardinal Primate of his diocese but he felt the sacrifice was worth it.

Dipheko had seen Jesus as a revolutionary, but one who depended totally for his success on non-violence. Camilo Torres represents a growing number of priests and dedicated lay people who, in Latin America and in other parts of the world, have engaged in violent struggle with and on behalf of their struggling people.

Ernesto Cardenal stands in the same line as Torres. A poet, a contemplative and a writer, Cardenal attracts large audiences whenever he speaks in the world. He started his religious life under the direction of the Cistercian monk, Thomas Merton, and was told point blank by him to leave the cloistered life of Gethsemane monastery and become a contemplative among the peasant masses who dwelt on an archipelago in Nicaragua. He has this to say in his 'Letter on the Destruction of Solentiname':

Contemplation means union with God. We soon learnt (in our community at Solentiname) that this union with God was leading us to union with the very poor and abandoned peasant farmers who lived along the banks of the archipelago. The same contemplation soon led us to political engagement. Contemplation led us to revolution – and if it had been otherwise, it would have been false contemplation. My old novice master, Thomas Merton, had told me that in Latin America, contemplation could not be divorced from political struggle.

Cardenal concludes his statement by sharing with us the fact that the poor are our teachers and our liberators. He writes:

> If the Church isolates itself (from the poor) it no longer possesses the 'elan', the breath of the Spirit. Today the Church's mission among us all is to give its blessing to the kind of revolution that the Third World needs and longs for.[12]

But Jesus is bigger than the church and his appeal goes far beyond the confines of ecclesiastical buildings and institutional churches. The Christian has to be liberated from an individualistic interpretation of the Bible which has made God white, his concerns middle-class and his preferences linked with the perpetuation of the Western way of life. Western Christians must also be liberated from a non-political interpretation of the gospel which has reduced Jesus to a figure of sentimentality, stripped of his passion, moral strength and outspokeness. The pale, gentle-faced Jesus so endearing to our Victorian forebears and so out of keeping with the liberator image with which the oppressed see him, is rightly challenged, and not only by Christians. If the poor have something to teach us and share with us about their kind of Jesus, could a Marxist have anything to offer us? I am convinced he/she can. Jesus is not the sole prerogative of Christians only. Just as Dipheko from his vantage point of a cell in solitary confinement could discover Jesus as revolutionary, so there are others who ask the church to reject the larding-over process with which Western Christendom has altered the biblical image of the poor man from Nazareth. I am not speaking of a socialist Christ, any more than I can speak of a capitalist Christ. I am thinking more of the socialist who demands that proper attention and respect should be accorded those parts of Jesus' revolutionary message which the church has either muted, forgotten or ignored down through the ages. The church has presented Jesus in many different ways in the long course of its history. Is it not high time for him to be presented in all the strength and vitality of the Jesus who was prophet, defender of the poor, lover of the outcast?

The average person in the pew in Britain today, fed on an anti-Marxist diet and convinced of the totally oppressive nature of atheistic communism, would hardly be inclined to take seriously the proposition that a Marxist's view of Jesus had anything to teach him. He simply would not expect any Marxist to have a sympathetic view of Jesus at all. Yet Milan Machovec, the third example I have chosen, writing in a book called *A Marxist Looks at Jesus*, has some beautiful comments to make on our Lord's teaching which are not only helpful but challenging and instructive as well. There is a breaking process involved here. Our pride has to be broken so that we can be moved to admit that Christians do not have a monopoly on Christ: others can challenge our interpretation of the gospel. Writing in a chapter headed, 'The Significance of Jesus', he makes what for Western Christians sounds like an astonishing claim: 'Of his fullness we have all received.'[13] He affirms that Jesus 'has been confessed by great thinkers and simple people, rulers and martyrs and torturers'. Then comes the challenge to our complacency. Though he naturally admits the right of Catholics, Protestants and Orthodox to confess his name, he goes on to assert the right of Marxists, 'heretics and atheists', as he calls them, to do the same. He claims they have done more to advance the teaching of Jesus in its social dimensions than the churches. Herein lies his challenge to us. Is it true? Many Marxists, but also many critical modern theologians, are aware that concern for the future, the longing for liberation and radical change once found in Christianity, has been taken over in many countries by Marxists. What was true for Dipheko is also true of Machovec: he does not blame Christians for being disciples of Jesus, but for betraying his cause. They have, in fact, he asserts, become the modern Pharisees, condemned by the statement: 'This people honours me only with lip-service, while their hearts are far from me' (Mark 7.6).

So he quotes Marx addressing bourgeois Christians of his own time:

Does not every minute of your practical life give the lie to your theory? Do you consider it wrong to appeal to the courts when you are cheated? But the apostle writes that it is wrong. Do you offer your right cheek when struck on the left? Are not your court proceedings and the majority of civil laws concerned with property?

31

But you have been told that your treasure is not of this world?'[14]

Who can doubt from the church's failures in South Africa, Namibia and Rhodesia, from the appalling collaboration of the church with the ghastly dictatorships of Latin America, from the commercialization of religion in the United States, from the church's deafening silence and failure to act on behalf of the sufferings of oppressed people throughout the world that much of what Machovec says is both true and timely? When Christianity has been reduced only to a reform of the heart and when it declares it can do nothing about the state of the world, this is when it is exposed to its sharpest critics. Though he admits that the dogmatic image of Jesus has never been able fully to banish the image of the poor man of Nazareth, yet prophets and saints have had to fight against authoritarianism within the church to get that message across and have been exposed and hounded by 'the authoritarian guardians of dead conventions' in the process of so doing.

Women in today's church who have been verbally assaulted by Pauline texts that women should be silent in church; blacks whose forebears struggled with the demon of slavery and who themselves struggle with the violence of racism, will both be moved by Machovec's rejection of the Pauline message on the toleration of slavery. 'The words of Paul sound almost like a parody of the Jesus message. "Let all who are under the yoke of slavery regard their masters as all worthy of honour, so that the name of God and the teaching may not be defamed" (I Tim. 6.1) ... "Bid slaves to be submissive to their masters and to give satisfaction in every respect; they are not to be refractory" (Titus 2.9).'[15] Anyone who has seen the suffering of oppressed people knows that there has to be another alternative to that of meek submission. The point is not to accept the world but to change the world. This is the clarion call the Marxist makes to the contemporary Christian lulled into complicity with a false interpretation of scripture that tells oppressed people to put up with injustice and pie in the sky will be theirs by and by. The church today needs the fervour and the challenge of the socialist. Machovec, whose own people have come out of bitter poverty, knows that to tolerate it is sin. The verses of Psalm 72 which contain the messianic hope of the oppressed people capture for us the nature of the God

32

who shows no tolerance for tyrants or oppressors. Liberation, not toleration, is what is being offered:

> Uprightly he will defend the poorest, he will save the children of those in need, and crush their oppressors. (Ps. 72.4).

The gospel message of liberation must not be allowed to fall into the hands of the manipulative oppressor, so that liberation is postponed until some ever-diminishing point of distant eternity, or betrayed by insensitive theologians to be a mere liberation of the soul. The hungry, the worn out, the broken poor need their freedom now. They need to hear with Zacchaeus the liberating news, 'Today salvation has come to this house.' (Luke 19.9). Who can doubt that Machovec is right when he speaks of Jesus in the following way: 'But he was concerned with man, with his future and his present, his victories and failures, his love and pain, his despair and unconquerable hope.'[16]

It is this theme of unconquerable hope that is so manifest in the liberation struggles which both confront and challenge Christians in oppressive societies today. I made a free translation of a Spanish poem written by Edwin Castro, a political prisoner who was killed in a Nicaraguan gaol. His message is clear: Today's valleys of despair become tomorrow's rocks of hope.

> Tomorrow, son, it's going to be different.
> The prison door that closes
> on the anguished eyes
> of doomed men
> will be torn down.
> That peasant will fall on his knees
> and burst into laughter.
> That land is his –
> maybe it is small, but, by God,
> it belongs to him.
> All that hard work you talk about,
> why, that's a joke for him.
> The landless ones, all these poor peasants,
> will no longer have to sell

their children's bodies for a
thin slice of bread.
By the sweat of their own work
they'll feed and clothe every one.
No more will poor
people cry out
in the cold for a roof over
their heads.
Tomorrow, son, it's going to be great!
There'll be no imprisonment either
for daring to think,
or speak what's on your mind.
No lashing of backs,
no bullets aimed to make you
pause and
think again.
You, son, will walk
hand in hand with your kids
as I yearn to walk with you.
You won't spend your youth
behind bars, as I
have spent mine.
Exile won't claim your
corpse either. Nor will you freeze
to death, as you try to suck up the dust
of the powdered earth
as my father did when he died.
Tomorrow, son, I promise,
it's going to be different!

3

Climb Every Mountain

If my birth in Balfour Street left an indelible mark on me, deportation from Namibia left another. It has to be listed as the greatest trauma in my whole life, so that I literally think in terms of before deportation and after deportation. Namibia is quite unashamedly the obsession of my life. Its independence, the freedom of its people, the welfare of its oppressed masses at home or in exile are my chiefest concern. I think Namibia, pray Namibia, speak Namibia – yes, and literally dream Namibia. My dream has developed a monotony all its own: I am trying to get into the country only to be discovered by the police and arrested. So with the writer of Psalm 137 and with thousands of Namibian exiles I can affirm, 'Namibia, if I forget you, may my right hand wither! May I never speak again, if I forget you! If I do not count Namibia the greatest of my joys!' Exile has brought with it pain, frustration, despair, suffering and feelings of total impotence when reacting to the news that a priest has been imprisoned and tortured, one thousand Namibian students have been massacred by South African forces at Cassinga, mass arrests have taken place, SWAPO demonstrators have been beaten and tear gassed in Windhoek. Something of what Mary and the women who watched by the cross felt, I feel. Namibia's crucifixion is a via dolorosa, a death agony, with its daily procession of torture, shootings, imprisonments, deportations, and denials of the right of people to be free.

If it were only that, then the burden would be intolerable. But it quite definitely is not, as the following spiritual indicates:

> There'll be singin', there'll be singin',
> There'll be singin' over me,
> And before I'll be a slave,

> I'll be buried in my grave
> And go home to my Lord to be free.

In my freedom struggle there are dimensions which add a touch of glory to the struggle. Prisoners sentenced to twenty years on Robben Island sing, laugh and clap in court. Priests fined for illegal demonstrations crack jokes and laugh at the head of the security police when he enters the courtroom. A group of student exiles meeting with me in a classroom 6,000 miles from home break into a dance then hug and embrace me. 'These men are drunk with new wine' was the recorded verdict of onlookers at the first Pentecost. What will be the reaction to this the second? A new nation is being forged out of the pains and daily humiliations of the Namibian people. Rhetoric? Moonshine? Euphoric self-comforting? No, none of these. Anyone who has visited the SWAPO camps in Africa or has watched Namibian students will catch immediately the dynamic of a new creation. This is the new wine for the new Namibia.

What impact has the struggle in which I am engaged had upon my emerging theology? What aspects of the gospel speak to our need, help us cope with our situation? Well, above all, for us the gospel is first and last all about liberation. If it is not then it is nothing. Unless it can bring hope, speak of deliverance, depict God as rescuer of the afflicted, then it is useless to our need and will be cast off like the unclean rags of racism with which the oppressed Namibian people have been clothed for too long. The striking thing one notices about the oppressed is the urgency with which they lay claim to the biblical promises and the vigour with which they demand their implementation. One could contrast the pallid abstractions with which most Western Christians speak about God. In the same way the liturgy in most Western churches is passionless. You have to feel oppressed, smart under oppression and be striving to overthrow it before the full impact of the gospel message hits home: for the gospel is freedom.

Jesus is the sign of the kingdom. With his coming the reign of God's justice begins. Imagine the excitement with which a black congregation in the war zone in Northern Namibia would respond to Luke 4.18-19:

> The spirit of the Lord has been given to me,
> for he has anointed me.

He has sent me to bring the good news to the poor
to proclaim liberty to captives
and to the blind new sight,
to set the downtrodden free,
to proclaim the Lord's year of favour.

Jesus has been sent to the poor, the downtrodden, the captive: he has expressed a preference for them. Now this is the breaking process. What was true in his time is still true today. The poor receive the gospel with joy and amazement that God has a place, the most special place, for them. The rich, the powerful, those who would deem themselves 'religious' are sent empty away. The gospel produces conflict, just as Jesus brought conflict: 'Do not suppose that I have come to bring peace to the earth ... I have come to set a man against his father, a daughter against her mother, a daughter-in-law against her mother-in-law. A man's enemies will be those of his own household' (Matt. 10.34-36). Jesus sets in motion the breaking process. His disciples have to make certain choices: they must choose him before father or mother, husband or child. They must be prepared to leave all and follow him. They are called to lay down their life for him and the kingdom. The breaking process is clearly seen as a dying process too: a death to the old formalism of religion, a seeking first his kingdom and all that that implied. What did this process imply? Well, for those first disciples a greater freedom. They were freed from the shackles of religious scrupulosity, the tithing of herbs and salt, the spiritual arrogance of a religious elite, the violent judgments passed on sinners and non-illuminati. They were freed to love, to lay down their lives in service, freed from race, class and tribal taboo to see all men as their neighbour. Most of all they were liberated from greed and egoism and shown by example of one never-to-be-forgotten life that love is the greatest attribute of all. 'He had always loved those who were his in the world, but now he showed how perfect his love was' (John 13.1). The impact of that love can only be guessed at: they died rather than betray it.

Yet the thing about Jesus was you either loved him or hated him; you followed him or plotted to kill him. Jesus really did tear apart his own society by his words, by his actions, by those with whom he associated, including harlots and some extremely unsavoury charac-

37

ters. Everything about him invited confrontation and the scribes, the Pharisees, the chief priests, the elders of the people set out to get him. There was nothing of the appeaser about Jesus. He did not practise the art of religious diplomacy. His language too showed no restraint; though it shone with gentleness and compassion for the sick, the broken, the rejected and unwanted, it carried all the sting of the viper when it was exposing the religious hypocrisy of the Pharisees and the cold vanity of ecclesiastical swaggering that revelled at the greetings in the market place or the exalted seat at high table. Society's values were being exposed to the fierce gaze of the prophet, were broken in pieces to be replaced by the demand for total, self-giving love.

No one reading the gospel honestly could come away with a different conclusion: Jesus challenged the society of his day, exposed its meanness and sought to replace it. He was killed for so doing. Moreover, he never sought to apologize for this confrontation: he saw it as an inevitable consequence of faithfulness to the gospel. It was, in fact, something his disciples ought to expect, indeed rejoice over whenever and wherever it happened. 'Happy are you when people abuse you and persecute you and speak all kinds of calumny against you on my account. Rejoice and be glad, for your reward will be great in heaven; this is how they persecuted the prophets before you' (Matt. 5.11,12). Just to stress the point Luke in his gospel adds the words, 'dance for joy' when Christians were so abused or named as criminals. He goes even further in contrasting the lot of the rich against the blessedness of the poor.

Alas for you who are rich: you are having your consolation now.
Alas for you who have your fill now: you shall go hungry.
Alas for you who laugh now: you shall mourn and weep.
Alas for you when the world speaks well of you! This was the way their ancestors treated the false prophets (Luke 6.24-26).

It is clear for whom Jesus reserved his blessings and equally clear for whom he released his wrath. In her liberation canticle the Virgin Mary sums it all up fairly simply: 'the rich he has sent empty away' (Luke 1.53). Now this drives most Western churchmen mad. It is simply an absurdity, they claim, that God deals thus with rich people. The thought runs clear contrary to logic, it is offensive to think of the number of our friends, all kind, nice, generous-hearted people in their way, who would be excluded if this statement were taken at its face value. 'God loves rich people too!' becomes the strident, aggressive clarion call. It goes further: in the rich churches of the West it has become part of a theological crusade, so much so that written on the American dollar are the words, 'In God we trust,' lest we forget that God loves the rich just as much as he loves the poor. Now, in my travels throughout the world, I find another characteristic of this Western God. When I speak of the sufferings of the poor, when I speak of the recent victims of South Africa's violent aggression, it regularly happens that in the prayers which follow my sermon, the priest prays for the oppressor with the same urgency as he does for the oppressed. Now, whereas it is certainly true that in the Christian dispensation we are bidden to pray for our enemies and for those that despitefully use us, the speed with which this is done serves to remind me that the church goes overboard not to offend the rich. At its most extreme such posturing presents a God who is all things to all people. I find this idolatry: we have made a God in our own Western image and likeness. This God can tolerate the intolerable, put up with massacres, take in his stride genocide, accept starvation and disease caused by the ravages of hunger and still keep his cool. Such a God is a monster and is totally alien to scripture. He is the creation of the rich man, and is wheeled out to bless stock exchange dinners and the junketing of banana-republic military dictators. His priests are used to say benedictions over the guns of the tyrants and to admonish the poor and wretched to turn the other cheek. We have reduced the living God to an idol by making him conform to our outrages and violences and to pronounce them innocent and good. When this happens apostasy has taken place evidenced from the fact that the poor are the ones that have been sent empty away from our churches.

Jesus stands in the line of the prophets and as such proclaims the inalienable rights of the poor as God's specially loved and chosen ones. The God he represents and whose cause he maintains is readily recognizable in the pages of the Bible. He storms through the pages of history as the enemy of tyrants, the condemner of the exploiter, the one who bears an implacable hostility to the perpetrators of violence against the poor, the weak and the helpless. He is renowned as the one who takes up the cause of the widow, the orphan and the stranger. He does not overlook the iniquities of the mighty against the powerless: human memory may fail but God remembers. As such his true nature and character are blazoned forth at the beginning of Hebrew law: 'I am the Lord your God who brought you out of the land of Egypt and out of the house of bondage.' Because he rescued Israel from slavery, so he punished them through capitivity when they in turn forgot him and enslaved others.

Now in situations of political or racial turmoil and conflict, it is surprising and shocking how often the church has forgotten the true demands of the gospel, has forsaken her theology and has substituted a time-serving policy of neutralism, non-involvement, a count-me-out style of existence. In a society such as exists in Namibia today, which is tearing itself apart in civil war, the majority of churches have been happy to go along with the official policies of the South African government, so long as they are left free to do what most churches do: marry, baptize, hold services, run youth and Sunday school groups. But judged by the words of scripture, such seemingly innocent pastimes have the stroke of doom hanging over them now as then: '... people were eating and drinking, taking wives, taking husbands, right up to the day Noah went into the ark, and they suspected nothing till the Flood came and swept all away' (Matt. 24.38,39). The rich here had commandeered the church, determined her priorities and were happy that things were as they were. Poverty, the cruel laws of apartheid bit savagely into the heart of the black people, but what had all this to do with religion? The parish outing, choir practice, the dedicated giving campaign, all this was what it meant to be about their father's business. The weightier matters of the law – justice, mercy, good faith (Matt. 23.23) found no mention in their sermons or their liturgy – as conspicuously absent from them as they were from their daily lives. If asked why this was so, they would have rigorously replied, the church must have nothing to do with politics, and would quote that Jesus was a spiritual figure who had refused the appeal of the Zealots, had avoided the political arena by refusing to be crowned king, and by averring, 'Mine is not a kingdom of this world' (John 18.36). In fact, the less their gospel had to say about the present Namibian situation, the more proud they were of it. 'We don't need politics in church,' I was told by a devout member of the cathedral, 'we need more spirituality.' It was perfectly useless my replying, 'this is what Yahweh asks of you: only this, to act justly, to love tenderly and to walk humbly with your God' (Micah 6.8), because she had already 'spiritualized' that process which for her meant literally giving food parcels from time to time to African workers, sending alms to the missions, and going to mass twice a week.

God will understand her position, Western mentors advise me. After all, she is an old woman and of her to whom little is given, little will be expected! But this misses the point: the fact is that whole churches throughout the world have reduced the gospel to the dimension of trivia. We allow people to substitute a few coins in a mission box instead of demanding the justice that the Bible requires for the oppressed. Instead of that total involvement in the suffering of those injured by the injustices of society, as shown in the parable of the Good Samaritan, we allow the wishy-washiness of what passes for intercessory prayer which so often comes out like, 'God bless everybody, Amen.' Such posturing is deadly as far as the spiritual well-being of the rich is concerned; but is it no less lethal in its effects on the poor? For them it is intolerable.

Jesus passed a sevenfold indictment against the Pharisees: it holds just as good for us today. 'Alas for you, scribes and Pharisees, you hypocrites! You who shut up the kingdom of heaven in men's faces, neither going in yourselves nor allowing others to go in who want to' (Matt. 23.13). Neither going in yourselves nor allowing others to go in – that is the agony of Namibia. Whites who opt for a gospel which excludes justice for the poor, and is therefore idolatry, the ignoring of the true God and the worshipping of one's own projected ego, values and prejudices, not only reject the kingdom, but prevent others from seeking it, in this instance, through the medium of the church. This is a double curse. Not that I believe their action can block the oppressed from forwarding the justice that God is seeking, for God has other means than the church to do this.

A second development occurs in a situation of conflict. Jesus said, 'He who is not with me is against me' (Matt. 12.30). We have described the situation of so-called a-political Christians who adopt a neutralist stance in areas of conflict, but these are rarely meek and mild. Your protagonist of the gentle Jesus meek and mild gospel is rarely meek and mild when dealing with those whom he believes threaten his theology. In fact, he is usually downright violent! Those who began by approving the gracious words which flowed from the

Lord's mouth (Luke 4.22) were so enraged at the end of his sermon that they wanted to throw him over the edge of a cliff (Luke 4.28-30). There is no greater fanatic than the religious fanatic, no matter how benign his smile nor warm his welcome on first acquaintance. Empires have been built on false gods and those that espouse them are not grateful when their kingdoms stand in danger of being over-thrown. Fleshpots are still fleshpots whether they exist in Egypt, London, New York, Johannesburg, Canterbury or Rome. They will always say of those who seek to implement the liberative aspects of Jesus' teaching, 'The man casts out devils only through Beelzebub, the prince of devils' (Matt. 12.24). A whole series of criticism is levelled against those Christians who stand in solidarity with the oppressed and most of it is aimed at destroying their character. So they are depicted by conservative Christians as political, emotional, haters of the rich, class-conscious, envious, publicity seekers, and that all-purpose knock-out word, communists! Easier by far to say Jesus is mad than to examine the justice of his claims. Devastating to say he does good by using evil methods for no argument can defend that. 'If they persecuted me, they will persecute you too' (John 15.20).

The injustice in Namibia and South Africa galls and is indefensible; then why have the majority of churches done so little effectively to change the minds and attitudes of whites in that society which more than any other claims to be Christian? South Africa, like Ireland, has one of the highest rates for church attendance in the world. Why is it then that the gospel has had so little impact on the lives and racial attitudes of the white people? The answer is of course that 'a gospel' has had a staggering effect on the lives of the white community, just as it has had an effect on the lives of middle-class white Anglo-Saxon Americans, on middle-class German businessmen, on middle-class Swiss bankers, and middle-class members of London's stock exchange. But that 'gospel' was not the gospel of Jesus Christ. It was a gospel tailor-made to keep in complacent comfort those who espoused it and who financially supported it, but it is clearly another gospel and as such is to be condemned. For as Paul testified, 'if anyone preaches a version of the Good News different from the one we have already preached to you, whether it be ourselves or an angel from heaven, let him be condemned' (Gal. 1.8).

How shall we characterize this 'other gospel', the gospel of the rich?

Well, first of all, it has changed the whole character of God: God is not the one who liberates, who overthrows oppressors, who demands justice of the rich towards the poor, restitution of what was stolen from the weak or helpless, the upholding of the cause of the oppressed, the God who makes urgent demands on his children so that a just society should be attained here on earth as in heaven. The whole character of God has been mutilated: God helps him who helps himself, the weakest go to the wall, charity begins at home. He is the god who calls unclean what God has cleansed, who segregates and ghettoizes those whom God would join together, who accepts sacrifices without mercy and holocausts without justice.

The voice of God which of old time spoke to our forefathers through the prophets (Heb. 1.1), which roared from Zion (Amos 1.2), declaimed against kings (II Sam. 12.7-10), overthrew governments, displaced nations and challenged the whole earth (Isa. 1.2) has been replaced by the banality of the chaplain's half-hour, the little talk with Jesus that puts it right, and such earth-shattering questions as 'Do pussycats go to heaven!' Is not the judgment of the apostle Paul reserved for such? (Rom. 1.18).

Worse still has happened. Instead of the gospel liberating men and women into becoming 'heirs of God and co-heirs with Christ' (Rom. 8.17), this alter-gospel has enchained the church in a Babylonian captivity to the standards and prejudices of a rotten society. The god so worshipped is an oppressor who tolerates all the abominations that abound in a racist society. The God who is known through the revelation of history as the liberator of the oppressed has been transformed: he is just as enslaved to the passions of this world as his followers are. He is a false god of whom it can be written, 'I am the Lord your God who dragged you into the land of Egypt and held you in the house of bondage. You shall have as many false gods as me.'

It is this false god of white oppression whom blacks in Namibia and South Africa have turned against and reject. I have said that unless the gospel is about liberation the poor will rightly reject it as an irrelevance. But in which churches can the poor see this gospel being proclaimed? For them theology must meet the agony in their heart, the hunger in their belly, the sense of deadness they feel on encountering the white man's God. Deliverance must be seen as God's initiative, as effective today as the Bible claims it was at the time of the exodus from Egypt. The God who then saw 'the miserable state of my people' (Ex.3.7ff.), heard 'their appeal to be free from their slave drivers', was 'well aware of their sufferings', was determined 'to deliver them out of the hands of the Egyptians' had a destiny planned for them which included placing them in 'a land where milk and honey flow'. The nature of this God, which again is further emphasized in the continuation of the Exodus passage just quoted, stresses beyond question of doubt the nature of God whom the oppressed saw and to whom they responded: he is the one who always hears the cry of the oppressed (Ex.3.9), who clearly sees what the oppressor is doing (Ex.3.9), and who acts on their behalf by raising up a saviour: 'I send *you* to Pharoah to bring the sons of Israel out of Egypt' (Ex.3.10).

Now it is this last aspect that the 'white' idolator questions: he questions the saviour whom God always sends to the assistance of the oppressed. Because he has tolerated the intolerable for so long, lived with an easy conscience among all the suffering daily experienced by the oppressed, dissociated his religious practices from the weightier things of mercy and justice, he has become a blind leader of the blind, he knows not the time of his visitation, he fails to recognize the hour of release from his bondage, that of oppressing others. He has got used to his chains. He is the one who tells the prophet to prophesy elsewhere and not disturb the *status quo*. 'Go away, seer; get back to the land of Judah; earn your bread there, do your prophesying there. We want no more prophesying in Bethel; this is the royal sanctuary, the national temple' (Amos 7.12).

So the zeal of the prophet is reduced to impotency by aggressive disbelief: '"Where did the man get all this!" ... And they would not accept him ... he could work no miracles there ... He was amazed at their lack of faith' (Mark 6.2ff.). The process is completely biblical: blinded by their idol, the people turn against God, slavery is the end-result. 'The Israelites did what displeases Yahweh. They forgot Yahweh their God and served the Baals and Asherahs. Then Yahweh's anger flamed out against Israel: he handed them over to Cushan-rishathaim the king of Edom, and the Israelites were enslaved ... for eight years' (Judg.3.7,8).

The process is re-enacted in the church repeatedly. Two examples will suffice. In Chile the church attempted to preserve a neutralist position both during and after the time of Allende. Because of its basic fear of socialism and because of a false feeling that it should not be seen as being 'involved in politics', it would not give wholehearted support for Allende's government. So on 27 May 1971, the bishops of Chile issued a working document, *Evangelio, politica y socialismo* in which they declared, 'The Church does not choose between different human groups. In and with Jesus Christ, the Church decides in favour of those whom Jesus decided in favour of: in favour of all the people of Chile.'[1] At first sight all the statement says is Jesus was on the side of people. But further examination bears out the absurdity of such a vague remark: Jesus condemned the Pharisees, called Herod a fox, slated religious hypocrisy, flung out the bankers from the Temple. The bishops are clearly presenting to the world their kind of Jesus, who is an historical absurdity – he just did not exist in the form they are describing. This is clearly an instance where bad theology makes for bad relations with the poor and the oppressed. If Jesus took sides, as he clearly did, then so must his church if it is to be the bringer in of his kingdom and if it is to remain true to his teaching. To say the church is for all the people of Chile is worse than meaningless, it is downright deceptive. Could the same be said at the time of Adolf Hitler? The church is in favour of all the people of Germany. Would the same proposition hold true for South Africa under the sway of an apartheid regime, or Namibia suffering the violence of the Administrator General's jackboot? By making such statements the church has reduced the God of the Bible to a marshmallow, and this is precisely what nauseates the struggling poor in such situations. This insipid, passionless church has produced a god to its own taste and liking. He is a god who slumbers while his people die in slavery or he has other priorities or preoccupations (I Kings 18.27).

In Namibia white Christians, whilst voting solidly for the *status quo*, the retention of the South African army, the liberalizing of a few racist laws, nevertheless strongly condemn what they describe as 'the terrorism' of SWAPO. For over one hundred years blacks in Namibia have suffered from a succession of cruel racist regimes. They survived the war of genocide unleashed on them, by the troops of the German General von Trotha's army, at the beginning of this century. They witnessed the annexation of their land and appropriation of their cattle under the Smuts regime in between the two world wars. From 1948 onwards they have suffered the cruel implementation of all the apartheid legislation which has denied them freedom of movement, expression, education and work. The apartheid society which has been inflicted on them violates every single principle of the Universal Declaration of Human Rights. Torture is practised, mass arrests are common, deportation of Christian missionaries is a regular feature of this regime, yet the white dominated churches, with one or two brave exceptions, have gone tamely along with all this. For one hundred years the oppressed Namibian people have reeled under successive and increasing waves of violence. Yet the appalling silence and complicity of white Christians will surely rank as one of the scandals of the twentieth century. Not only have white Christians been silent but they have become violent against any who raise their voice in protest, be they black or white. Yet the church is to be the herald of the kingdom. In 1978 my church issued a declaration on behalf of the oppressed. Having been deported from Namibia in 1972, I was not able to meet with my clergy and other church delegates there, but had to travel to the tiny mountainous kingdom of Lesotho to discuss there what we felt was the imperative of the Christian gospel for our country at that time. The result was the manifesto called *The Maseru Declaration*.

We saw the activity of the five Western powers, who were claiming they were trying to break the deadlock between South Africa and the United Nations, as greatly favouring South Africa, and giving her time to extend further her military and political control over Namibia. We said so in strong unequivocal language. Two years later the force of what we said is even more true:

> We see the Western intentions as being based on greed – aimed primarily at securing their continuing exploitation of Namibia's mineral wealth. We also see the five Western Powers blatantly attempting to coerce those forces which are working for the true liberation of our country and believe that their actions have done little to achieve basic changes in South Africa's policies and the structures of Namibian society.

> The Anglican Church, along with other Churches, deplores the mass slaughter of innocent men, women and children at Cassinga and elsewhere, and offers its deepest condolences to all those who have been thus bereaved, including our brethren from the

Lutheran Church, Bishop Leonard Auala, Pastor Cleopas Dumeni, and others who lost loved ones in the massacre. The names of our dead will be added to the long list of those who have lost their lives in the struggle for a free Namibia.

We, the delegates at the Maseru Conference, reaffirm our Church's commitment to the Gospel of Jesus Christ which speaks of freedom, justice and the worth of every human being. We see two forces at work in Namibia: the oppressive force of the South African regime and those who cooperate with it and, opposing them, the forces representing the poor and the oppressed people of Namibia.

In this confrontation there can be no place for neutrality. The Church has to decide with which side she should stand. We wish to make our choice clear before the eyes of the world. We see Jesus himself poor, and rejected by the oppressive forces of his day, taking his stand on the side of the poor and oppressed: we in Namibia can do no less.

Therefore, we appeal to all Churches and members of the international community to continue to help us and all others who are providing funds for the defence of political prisoners in Namibia, to assist us as we care for their families. In Namibia we see Jesus in our midst in many forms – in the poor, in the despised, the hungry, the wretched, the tortured, and in the political prisoner. Moved by the deepest feelings of compassion, we believe that true justice demands the release of all Namibian political prisoners held on Robben Island and in other prisons by South Africa.

We wish to make known to the world the continuing indiscriminate use of torture by the South African regime in Namibia. We see the failure to make effective protest against the use of torture as a moral weakness; we, for our part, will continue to protest so long as its use continues in our land. We stand with those Churches and individuals in Namibia who protest against the use of torture, and are grateful to such groups as Amnesty International for their unwavering support for the victims of South African violence.

We recognize the Church by its own efforts cannot achieve political and economic liberation and independence of our country, but we claim the right to identify and give support to those forces which

47

can. In this respect we support the efforts of those countries in the United Nations who, upholding the findings of International Law, are supportive of the liberation struggle in Namibia.

Though we have seen the deportation of three bishops of the Anglican Church, the daily harassment of our clergy and people, the hostility and violence of the occupying regime against us, we assert our right as Christians to speak out against such violence as conscience and the law of God demand.

God, who in the Bible identifies himself with the oppressed and firmly opposes the oppressor, demands that we, his servants, should also make our stand with all in our country who are oppressed, exploited, despised, harassed, intimidated, in prison for political offences or arbitrarily tortured for reasons of conscience, by a regime which, to sustain itself, is increasingly resorting to violence.

At a time when the unity of the oppressed is essential, we are opposed to any attempts, internally or externally, which seek to weaken that unity. There is one struggle of the oppressed people, just as there will be one victory.

To those governments and institutions who have offered scholarships and training programmes or domicile to Namibians in exile, we offer our grateful thanks. Finally, we rejoice that God has called us to witness to his redeeming and liberating love through sharing the suffering of the oppressed. In his strength we shall continue to strive for the final liberation of our country from the evils of racism and oppression which now hold us in bondage.

Reconciliation will only come to Namibia when true justice is accorded to the oppressed. As we work for that liberation we acclaim God the Holy Spirit who Himself has inspired all the oppressed with the freedom to be free. [2]

It was clear from its reception that this was a highly controversial document. Only a handful of white Christians in our church would agree with it, let alone subscribe to it. Its publication was the immediate cause of the deportation of the Vicar General, Ed Morrow, his wife, Laureen, and their daughter, Lydia. 'Moderate' white church people in the Republic of South Africa would regard its publication as provocative, sensational and aggressive. It would be yet another case of the Anglican Church in Namibia sticking its neck out, asking for trouble and getting it. The document has been given worldwide coverage and history will judge both its importance and effectiveness. For me here was an instance where the oppressed dared stand up and say, 'thus saith the Lord'. Our document was rejected by the whites in our church because it was an affront on their type of Christianity. We were asking them to change and this they were clearly not prepared to do. They saw us as wanting to overthrow their world and they were right. For, with a commitment to change, goes a commitment to change theology, and both are dangerous for affluent people.

So rejection is clearly one obvious aspect of the breaking process. In the ministry of Jesus, as recorded in the gospels, it is a recurring and painful experience. Nazareth rejects him, cutting him down to size in a vicious way by questioning the legitimacy of his birth: 'This is the carpenter, surely, the son of Mary ...' (Mark 6.3). Jerusalem reduces him to tears by its obduracy: 'As he drew near and came in sight of the city he shed tears over it' (Luke 19.41-44). He who could restore sight to the blind (Luke 18.35-43) was rendered helpless at the stubborness of the spiritually benighted men preferring darkness to light (John 3.19). What broke Jesus must surely break us (John 15.20). But the breaking process does not end with Jesus' humiliation: it concludes with his victory. The disciples did not go forth into the wide world to proclaim a failure, they were the heralds of a victory. The way this victory is to be achieved has riven asunder Western Christendom.

The clear-cut message of the book of Judges, which deals with a time of near enslavement and oppression, is plainly this: 'When the Israelites cried to Yahweh because of Midian, Yahweh sent a prophet to the Israelites. This was the message, "Thus Yahweh speaks, the God of Israel. It was I who brought you out of Egypt and led you out of a house of slavery. I rescued you from the power of the Egyptians and the power of all who oppressed you. I drove them out before you and gave you their land, and I said to you: I am Yahweh your God. Do not reverence the gods of the Amorites in whose land you now live. But you have not listened to my words" ' (Judg. 6.7-10).

Moses was clearly a man driven on by an obsession – the attainment of the Promised Land for his people. Though he never made it there himself, yet there were moments of glory for this man whom 'Yahweh knew face to face' (Deut. 34.10). And so too will it be for those who, like him, struggle with a people who are marching to achieve the destiny God has prepared for them. Like Martin Luther King, they can exclaim, 'I may not make it with you to the promised land, but I have been on the mountain.' This too is part of the breaking process which, even though only once and perhaps dimly glimpsed, makes the struggle all the more compelling.

But what of those ordinary Christians who exist in their thousands, who struggle to be faithful to churches that have sold out the poor, lost the vision of justice for the oppressed, and suffocate under joyless services that seem to be leading to death rather than to resurrection. What hope exists for them? Are they totally abandoned? Where is the Moses-like vision for them? *A Falling Star* may speak to them.

A FALLING STAR

There are
trembling moments
ecstasy filled
when light gently parts
the hanging
dangling
down drifting
leaves of forest
trees
and as by instinct
you lift your face
towards the sun's
warmth and feel
within you
the heaving motion
of the forest
moving yet never
stirring filling
out the air you
breathe with the
power force that
once released creation
all silence
surrounded you
wait expectant
straining to hear
god walking in the
cooler air of the
day and as you
turn away you
feel more alone
than ever the trees
will go on swaying

disseminating
light and shadow
dropping endless
leaves of silence
onto the forest
floor
the branch that
seemed to quiver
with excitement as
you thrust it
back trembles
recoils and
watches reproachful
as your foot
prints vanish
in the parted
grass
eternity has
turned tail
toppled backwards
realing
over and over
like wind blown
tumble weed
and hidden there
within the
whisps and fronds
a hazel seed
that just
might tell you
things that
angels dare not
mention.

4

There's Gonna be a Great Day

'If I read the New Testament correctly,' writes James Cone, 'the resurrection of Christ means that he is also present today in the midst of all societies effecting his *liberation of the oppressed*. He is not confined to the first century, and thus our talk of him in the past is important only insofar as it leads us to an *encounter* with him *now*. As a black theologian I want to know what God's revelation means right now as the black community participates in the struggle for liberation.'[1]

For most Western Christians the implications of Jesus' death and resurrection would be a hereafter thing: heaven restored, a future life made possible with him in eternity, the sting of death removed, the promise that life does not come to an abrupt end with death. '"Your brother will rise again" ... "I know he will rise again at the resurrection on the last day"' (John 11.24,25) – the happening is thought of very much as a future thing. But for Cone, as expressed in this passage at least, it is a here and now event: Jesus is working now among oppressed people for their liberation. White churches remove all the urgency out of the salvation process, first by counselling patience to struggling, oppressed people: these things cannot be done over night, it all takes time, Rome was not built in a day, be patient. The black oppressed community reply, 'We want our freedom *now*.' Yet the New Testament shows the kingdom bursting in on the world with the coming of Jesus: 'But if it is through the finger of God that I cast out devils, then know that the kingdom of God has overtaken you' (Luke 11.20). Much of the passion has gone out of white Christianity simply because the impact of salvation has been deferred: it's a pie in the sky by and by which turns nobody on. The white Western affluent Christian has tamed the God of Moses who 'has covered himself in glory' (Ex. 15.1). You have to be oppressed to know this God in all his splendour. A people rescued from the jaws of death, plucked from seemingly endless slavery, they know how to respond to him, because they have experienced his deliverance. This is how they sang about that deliverance:

> 'Yahweh is my strength, my song,
> he is my salvation.
> This is my God. I praise him:
> the God of my father, I extol him' (Ex. 15.2).

Now if the poor have the gospel preached to them (Matt. 11.5) and if they enter the Kingdom before the righteous, it is they who can interpret it to their rich and more complacent neighbours, because they have caught the urgency of its appeal. We in Britain need to be open to all that the poor have to say to us.

Few white Christians in the United Kingdom today would speak euphorically about the World Council of Churches, let alone acknowledge that it is to be 'commended for its gesture of love, concern and compassion in coming to the aid of the struggling masses of our world.' Many Christians here would reject with indignation the claim by the same writer that 'The WCC Programme to Combat Racism, for example, is a visible expression of Christian love.' In fact, rage and anger would erupt in many Christian assemblies in Britain were these words, written by the present President of Zimbabwe, the Reverend Canaan Banana, to be addressed to their august meetings. The South African Department of Information has done its job extremely well and many Christians in Britain have responded to its propaganda efforts by condemning the freedom fighters as terrorists and deploring the WCC as a pro-communist organization and one that is supporting violence against Christian governments in Southern Africa. Yet the struggling poor in these countries who are the victims of white racism have been unflagging in their support for the Programme to Combat Racism and would completely agree with President Banana's comments that 'It (the PCR) is viewed by the oppressed as a grain of hope and comfort to many who would otherwise have died of hunger and from wounds inflicted by the bombs and guns of desperate enemies of freedom.' The breaking process is again at work. We either re-think our positions, assisted by the experience and sufferings of the struggling poor, or else we compound our prejudices by rejecting them for whatever reason seems best to us. But the testimony of such people as President Banana cannot be lightly dismissed and the South African propagandists in our midst will have to work even harder to refute the testimony of the oppressed. Canaan Banana goes further: he challenges the sub-structures of our Western belief when he writes: 'The quest for salvation is a quest for economic, political, social, and spiritual justice. Meaningful faith, therefore, must take place within the context of the total human situation.'[2]

The President is on firm ground for today he can point to the liberation process which has taken place and is still continuing in Zimbabwe. Against all the odds, and in total contradiction of all the predictions, the freedom movement of Robert Mugabe, president of ZANU, won a handsome victory. South Africa has still not recovered from the shock. Moreover, the British press failed completely to inform its readers or adequately prepare them for the result. What has shaken the world almost as much as the victory is the eirenic qualities of the new prime minister and the incoming regime. The takeover has been done with an almost total absence of pique, bombast or recrimination; there has been no bloodbath of former white enemies done to death.

Prime Minister Mugabe's speech on the eve of independence was not merely a brilliant piece of oratory, it was also a signal to the nation that reconciling love was really to be implemented forthwith. The oppressed knew how to show mercy, restraint, forgiveness. Some still find this shocking and would have enjoyed a purge as proof of the black man's bestiality: they will be disappointed. It has not happened; Mugabe instead has shown clemency, magnanimity, as the following speech clearly shows:

Tomorrow we shall be celebrating the historic national event which our people have striven for nearly a century to achieve. Our people, young and old, men and women, black and white, living and dead, are, on this occasion, being brought together in a new form of national unity that makes them all Zimbabweans. Independence will bestow on us a new personality, a new sovereignty, a new future and perspective, and, indeed, a new history and a new past.

Tomorrow we are being born again; born again not as individuals but collectively as a people, nay, as a viable nation of Zimbabweans. Tomorrow is thus our birthday, the birthday of great Zimbabwe, and the birthday of its nation. Tomorrow, we shall cease to be men and women of the past and become men and women of the future. It's tomorrow then, not yesterday which bears our destiny.

As we become a new people we are called to be constructive, progressive and for ever forward-looking, for we cannot afford to be men of yesterday, backward-looking, retrogressive and destructive. Our new nation requires of every one of us to be a new man, with a new mind, a new heart and a new spirit. Our new mind must have a new vision and our new hearts a new love that spurns hate, and a new spirit that must unite and not divide. This to me is the human essence that must form the core of our political change and national independence.

Henceforth, you and I must strive to adapt ourselves, intellectually and spiritually, to the reality of our political change and relate to each other as brothers bound one to another by a bond of national comradeship. If yesterday I fought you as an enemy, today you have become a friend and ally with the same national interest, loyalty, rights and duties as myself. If yesterday you hated me, today you cannot avoid the love that binds you to me and me to you. Is it not folly, therefore, that in these circumstances anybody should seek to revive the wounds and grievances of the past? The wrongs of the past must now stand forgiven and forgotten.

If ever we look to the past, let us do so for the lesson the past has taught us, namely that oppression and racism are iniquities that must never again find scope in our political and social system. It could never be a correct justification that because the whites oppressed us yesterday when they had power, the blacks must oppress them today because they have power. An evil remains an evil whether practised by white against black or by black against white. Our majority rule could easily turn into inhuman rule if we oppressed, persecuted or harassed those who do not look or think like the majority of us.

Democracy is never mob-rule. It is and should remain disciplined rule requiring compliance with the law and social rules. Our Independence must thus not be construed as an instrument vesting individuals or groups of individuals with the right to harass and intimidate others into acting against their will. It is not the right to negate the freedom of others to think and act as they desire. I, therefore, wish to appeal to all of you to respect each other and act in promotion of national unity rather than in negation of that unity.'[3]

There was a breaking process behind such words. Prime Minister Mugabe had been in prisons for eleven years, had been prevented by the Smith regime from attending the funeral of his own child, had suffered as so many of his comrades had suffered through the loss of freedom, through exile, through torture, through hunger, through daily humiliation. Such people's characters have been refined through the painful process of suffering. These words are not the mob oratory of the demagogue, nor do they reveal the political actor playing on the world stage. Those who know Robert Mugabe and are close to him are convinced that he is a living embodiment of what he says.

During the Zimbabwe independence celebrations I was able to have an interview with Garfield Todd, a previous Prime Minister of Rhodesia, who himself had been imprisoned, along with his daughter Judith, by the Ian Smith regime. I asked him for his opinion of Prime Minister Mugabe in the light of his pre-independence speech. 'Can you trust him?' I asked. 'Yes I do', he replied. 'I have a great estimation of the Prime Minister. Some whites are being cynical and the testing of his words will take time. I had Mr Mugabe as a teacher for a year on my farm. Consider his training at school, his Christian background and the influence of Father O'Haye, an Irish Catholic priest. I think we are very fortunate to have a man cradled in Christianity as is the new Prime Minister.'

Zimbabwe will rise from the ruins that a despotic racism led her to and under his leadership is trying to arise as a healed nation. Those churches and church leaders who denied this, withdrew or cancelled their support for the WCC Programme to Combat Racism, should now make public admission that they were wrong and should increase their previous contributions as a sign of the genuineness of their repentence. Guilty silences neither enhance the cause of Christianity nor make it more palatable to the struggling African people who feel betrayed by the indignant finger-pointing and posturing of such churches. It would help alleviate hurt feelings and put straight the record if these churches would now have the grace to come forward and admit that they were wrong.

So the liberation struggle in Southern Africa continues in Namibia and South Africa and Christians in the rest of the world are called to take sides. They are asked to make a conscious stand with the oppressed. The occasional declaration that they are against apartheid is clearly hardly sufficient: it is like a bishop saying he is against sin. A clear stand is what is called for which ought to be backed by financial and moral support. This can only come if there is intensive dialogue with the oppressed themselves. The leaders of the churches in Britain, Europe and North America ought to have meetings and discussions with the heads of the liberation movements or how else will they be able to understand the struggle of the oppressed? Furthermore, how can they possibly give the vital lead that is needed so that the white churches in Britain can repent of their racist tendencies? A true spirit of ecumenism means that the unity of the human race should be attained. This racism denies. Church unity is only a small part of world unity.

Africans in Southern Africa have repeatedly said that they do not hate whites because they are whites, but that they do hate racism and are determined to work for its overthrow. In the past, Western Christians have either disbelieved their leaders when they have said this or ignored them. Today, with the deliverance of Zimbabwe, they do so at their own peril. The monster of white racism has been slain in Zimbabwe and the task of real nation-building now begins. One does not underestimate the problems and difficulties facing the emerging state. One knows that the dragon's teeth of racist attitudes still linger on in the white civil service and elsewhere, but the people are at least now free to tackle their problems as a nation and will do so with vigour under a courageous leadership.

Despite all the birth pangs attending the arrival of the new emergent state can we not see that captives have been delivered from the bondage of white racism? Huge numbers of prisoners have been freed from their prisons – yes, though sad to say, a few have been re-imprisoned for crimes against their fellows. This does not detract from the overall liberation process. The poor are being cared for and given hope. The churches are involved in the construction of a new society. There has been a breaking process: a mighty act of liberation has taken place. Let Christians throughout the world thank God for it.

So what can British Christians learn from the Zimbabwean experience? I think the most important lesson is the determination of the oppressed to be free. Bankers in Britain who make rotating loans to the South African government, businessmen here who underpay their South African workers, forcing them to live in conditions of near starvation, governments who have baled out South Africa at the United Nations or have helped support her internationally, must know that the oppressed are absolutely determined to be free and when that freedom is attained they will remember who their friends were (and also who were their enemies). No sacrifice is too much for them to make and no struggle is too long for them to undergo. President Banana spelt this out clearly when he wrote the following when he was in prison:

> As for me, I am not ashamed of the revolution, for it is the power of the people unto salvation. I am grateful for the opportunity to participate in the humanizing struggle for our freedom. Although I continue to suffer imprisonment for my part in our struggle for social justice, I would consider my sacrifices as minute. Being personally involved in the struggles one cannot help being reminded again and again of the sacredness of human life. I have set the goal of freedom of my people above my highest joys. I would prefer to continue to suffer in gaol if the price demanded by my captors for my freedom is to renounce the cause for which countless Zimbabweans have sacrificed their precious lives. Indeed such an action would be treasonable. I cannot possibly sacrifice the legitimate aspirations of so many of our gallant comrades who have paid the supreme price for our freedom. They have died that we might live; they have lost their lives that we may find our own. I honour them. I salute them. A luta continua![4]

The world has witnessed an act of liberation in Zimbabwe where there has been an enactment of biblical themes: the mighty have been put down from their seat of privilege and vested power. The proud boasters that white is right have seen their godless racist theories laid low, but much more than this has been achieved. Liberation is not only the defeat of Pharaoh, in whatever guise he comes, it bestows on the oppressed their long denied heritage as true children of their heavenly father. The children of Israel were freed from the yoke of Pharaoh no longer to be slaves. The same is immediately obvious in Zimbabwe where a whole wind of change is blowing away from the minds of the oppressed past attitudes and mental blocks. It is of course early days but blacks are conscious of their new found freedom and are intoxicated by it. The mentality of the slave must be driven out with all the psychological destruction that accompanied it – the self-hate, the feeling of inferiority, the lack of self-confidence, the scorning of black culture. In Pauline language the black oppressed are now free 'to become what they already are'. But it took a revolutionary war to accomplish it. The freedom achieved in Zimbabwe was not handed gratuitously on a plate to the black people there: they were forced by white insensitivity, white greed, and white violence to die for it. It was bought at an immense cost by the black people. With the coming of that freedom certain 'signs' are already visible in the new Zimbabwe. The good news of liberation has reached the poor. A nation held captive by racism has been delivered from that particular scourge. Great and good men and women formerly placed in prison for reasons of conscience have been released and some whites who were themselves prisoners to an evil system now admit it was wrong – though amazingly enough I never met any white person whilst I was in Zimbabwe who actually said he had been a fervent supporter of Ian Smith! The oppressed rejoice in their new-found freedom. The question I ask myself is simply this: has the kingdom been advanced or retarded in Zimbabwe on this evidence?

There will be many who will say that the freedom won there is not absolute, that some feel excluded, that the nation is not completely united and others will add, how can you speak of the kingdom being advanced by means of a secular state? To these I would make the following comments. Jesus' death did not achieve immediate perfection in the human heart, but his redemption was open and offered to all. In Zimbabwe there is today an unquestionable potential for freedom far in advance of what was possible under the white regime. What is more, the churches are being used to build up the schools, clinics and homes of people broken by a war brought on by white racism. Surely the possibility for the kingdom's coming in Zimbabwe has been furthered? Moreover, it was not the church which brought about the great and fundamental changes so needed for the benefit of the nation's poor. Granted many Christians played a part in their personal capacity, but the church was not able to effect the change of a single oppressive law during the whole period of UDI. To me this is a clear instance that God has other instruments at his disposal through which he works his will. Let us as Christians graciously acknowledge that. More so, let us rejoice that the church's part in the struggle has been acknowledged by Robert Mugabe who has confidently placed so much faith in the churches in Zimbabwe and abroad to help build up his war ravaged country.

What we are today witnessing in Zimbabwe is undoubtedly a wonderful act of liberation. After one hundred years of colonial oppression, a people who were reduced to humiliating poverty and all the indignity and humiliation of being an occupied land, have now established their right to be free. Those who formerly were not a people have become a people with their country, their culture, their pride given back to them. The dead have been raised to life. For those of us who believe the kingdom of God is not coming in abstractions, are we not witnessing there what can truly be termed 'an acceptable year of the Lord'? In the light of Jesus' saying, 'The poor have the Gospel preached to them', are not the poor the ones who should be interpreting to us the salvic events in Zimbabwe rather than affluent Western theologians? The poor danced in the streets of Harare township with fronds in their hands singing out their hosannas to their God who had 'put down the mighty from their seat and had exalted the humble and meek'. If the Western Church were to challenge, 'Rebuke your disciples,' those of us who observed these independence celebrations could properly answer, 'The very stones of Zimbabwe would cry out.'

The church in the West must really try to see the mighty acts of God in contemporary society with the eyes of faith and modesty. If God chose Moses who was a former murderer, Aaron an idolator, Samson a playboy, David an adulterer, as instruments of deliverance for his people, should we today reject his acts of liberation unless these are led by popes, cardinals or bishops in ecclesiastical attire? Let not the church miss out and fail to recognize a deliverance when it occurs because it can only think in spiritual terms. If the poor are the first to benefit in God's kingdom, can not we as Christians rejoice that the victims of injustice, oppression and prolonged suffering in Zimbabwe now have a future bright with hope and brimful with possibilities now that their human dignity has once more been restored? Their oppressors too now have the opportunity of being humanized by being freed from the blind prejudices that made them oppressors in the first place. Jesus took up the theme and Luke portrays it with joy: Messianic justice for the oppressed was now bursting into the world through him and a divine revolution was actually happening. But this is not just to be interpreted as a theory: salvation takes place when we move from theory into actual living practice. Once again we must be liberated ourselves to see world events through the hope-filled eyes of the poor. Their eyes in Harare and Highfields townships were shining with real joy and that joy no one takes away from them. Like the Israelites of old they were laughing, dancing and singing in honour of the God who had in his mercy granted them a great deliverance.

The poor, we assert, are not one of the themes of the gospel, they are the very essence of the gospel. The fact that God always takes up their cause, the fact that their cause then becomes God's cause, is the clear message of the Bible. God does not want to see poverty continue, for it is the by-product of injustice, and he opposes it. But Jesus' kingdom divides (Matt. 10.34) and there can be no cosy relationships between oppressors and oppressed. God takes on the powerful when they exploit, he overthrows those who grind the faces of the poor in their search for power or wealth, for power is only acceptable when it defends justice. When it does not it becomes tyranny and must be overthrown. Just as those who wielded power unjustly in the time of Jesus maligned him as subversive, an overthrower of the state, a blasphemer, a plotter against Caesar, so today the church will be mercilessly attacked when it takes up the cause of the poor with courage and determination. Golgotha rears its head in such countries as Brazil, the Philippines, Chile, Namibia, South Africa to name just a few as the vested interests of the rich are threatened or exposed. Yet today as in the past, God manifests his solidarity with all those who hang on crosses and the church should be the first to acknowledge that Jesus exists in the lives of all those who take up the cause of the poor when they seek justice. The clear message of Good Friday is that

God does not allow the poor to die on their crosses for ever (Acts 2.32: God raised this man Jesus to life and all of us are witnesses to that). Though the rich declaim against those whom they hang on their crosses, they cannot take away from their victims that dignity in which God holds them: for to such people he has promised the kingdom (Matt. 5.10). Those who place people on crosses will not escape the judgment of God.[5]

Now much to the anguish of the poor, the church in the West regards all this as so much past history and, unlike James Cone, has little interest in what God is doing for the liberation of the oppressed here and now. Such attitudes reduce religion to an antiquarian study and its preachers to the condition of purveyors of harmless anecdotes. As far as Britain is concerned, what does it mean to proclaim the acceptable year of the Lord, the coming of God's kingdom?

Firstly, it places a demand on the proclaimer. 'We have seen the Lord' (John 20.25) was the watchword of the early disciples. The hallmark of their authenticity was the striking simplicity of their lives: 'No one claimed for his own use anything that he had, as everything they owned was held in common ... None of their members was ever in want' (Acts 4.32,34). It was through this that the early disciples 'continued to testify to the resurrection of the Lord Jesus' (Acts 4.33). Was it not through this simple, joy-filled sharing of poor people with other poor people that the truth of what they were saying convinced others? Their testimony to the resurrection was caring love: nothing else can replace this. Yet it is this lack of authentic love that is the most conspicuous in our church life. It is in loving that we are so sadly defective in the West.

What would it mean for bishops and archbishops to take up the cause of the poor here in Britain? One can mention some instances in which they do. I have before me a plea to the Church of England's General Synod in which Robert Runcie, the new Archbishop of Canterbury, appealed to the delegates to get their minds off a pre-occupation with liturgical reform, which they had been pursuing for the previous ten years, and deal with some of the burning social issues of the day. In this he was strongly supported by Simon Phipps, Bishop of Lincoln, and Stanley Booth-Clibborn, Bishop of Manchester, both of whose speeches were given sympathetic coverage in *The Guardian* newspaper.[6] I am sure these men are right to be offering this challenge to the Church of England at this time. I am also sure that it is not enough.

How are the poor faring in Britain in this last quarter of the twentieth century? If Professor Peter Townsend, in his recent book on *Poverty in the United Kingdom*,[7] is to be believed, the poor in this country are more plentiful than we ever believed. Yet, we have turned our faces from them, stuffed up our ears, and convinced ourselves, in words attributed to a leading politician, that 'there are no poor people in Britain today'. Professor Townsend's statistics, gathered over a period of ten years, suggest otherwise. Here are the facts that his study revealed – they will have since worsened: One in four persons in Britain is deprived or relatively deprived. Twenty per cent of old people are suffering from poverty and a further forty-four per cent are on the verge of poverty. Added to this, one million of these poor people fail to get the benefits which are legally theirs. The Professor's study shows that there is an enormous disparity between rich and poor in this country, a disparity which is as bad as anything that exists in the Third World. Five per cent of our population own a colossal forty-five per cent of this country's assets. When income is added to their already enormous wealth, the top ten per cent of people in Britain are ten times wealthier than the poorest ten per cent. So what was said about the injustice of the nineteenth century in a divided nation of rich and poor, still applies in Britain today. 'Our modern society that has sprouted from the ruins of the feudal society has not done away with class antagonisms. It has ... established new classes, new conditions of oppression, new forms of struggle in the place of the old ones.'[8] Add to this the fact that politicians who lead us have the effrontery to tolerate a situation where Britain's jobless unemployed have already gone beyond a level of two million and one is bound to ask, 'How can any church tolerate that?'

In other countries bishops are speaking out on behalf of the poor. Much coverage has been given to the visit of Pope John Paul II to Brazil. Some of his remarks are worth quoting. In Rio de Janeiro he is reported as saying, 'To hope that the solutions to problems of wages, social security and working conditions blossom as a kind of automatic extension of the economic order is not realistic and for that reason is not admissable. The economy will only be viable when it is human, made by and for man.'[9] When the Brazilian President, General

Figueredo, sought to restrict the function of the church to 'educating the young, aiding the needy, consoling those who suffer', the Pope hit back in an address to the President in which he emphasized that the priest's religious role contained 'a clear message about man, his values, his dignity and his life in society'. And in Rio de Janeiro, to the Latin American council of bishops, whose leadership is to the right, he had this to say, 'When the prostration of man is maintained or prolonged, the church denounces it. This is part of its prophetic service.'

The Pope was so moved by the plight of the poor in one area as to take off a golden ring from his hand and leave it behind as a gesture of goodwill, clearly shocked by what he had seen and experienced. But sincere and genuine as such gestures are, they can never eradicate the roots of the injustice which are the cause of the poverty. This must entail a correct socio-political analysis and a commitment to the liberation struggle. It is supremely here that those who respect the Pope for the dignity his office bestows, would be most critical both of his analysis and of his solutions. With five million abandoned children in Brazil, with a growing population today estimated at 120 million, the overwhelming majority of whom are desperately poor, the Pope reiterated his opposition to abortion as well as to artifical birth-control. But his Polish origins were as marked here as ever in his veiled reference to the possibility of revolutionary communism. His exact words were: 'To promote reforms in this way is also a way of avoiding that they be sought under the impulse of currents that do not hesitate to turn to violence and to the direct or indirect suppression of the rights and basic liberties inspired by the dignity of man.' One is tempted to ask what 'rights and basic dignities' the peasants and workers of Brazil enjoy at present under their military dictatorship and how that dictatorship can be changed to allow the starving people a life worthy of the name. Father Alipio de Freitas wrote about the military rulers of Brazil to his archbishop. He begins from a deep pastoral love and an intimate relationship with the people he serves, and writes as follows:

These are men who are fighting to prevent the country from developing and to impede all institutional reform, who lie to the working classes and keep wages down. They are the men who are now selling Brazil to the doubtful, indeed criminal, interests of international capitalism; they are the tools of imperialist domination, as they work to organize the Alliance for Progress, conspire against democracy and defend the privileges of the already over-privileged. They are the ravening wolves Christ spoke of who disguise themselves in sheep's clothing to get inside the fold. They have used their pastoral authority to condemn me for my support of the people, whom I love passionately, but whom they despise and hate. Your Eminence was bishop in the North and North-East of Brazil. You saw at close quarters the most appalling poverty, the most brutal exploitation, the most tragic socio-economic scene that anyone could witness. Having seen all that, Your Eminence should be able to understand the purpose and the significance of my struggle, with and for the people

The priest condemns the capitalist exploiters of the people but also condemns the hierarchy, an elite he calls them, whose reactionary attitudes scandalize him. In the light of his statement, what is required for a bishop to go through the breaking process? Fr Alipio spells it out to his archbishop:

But 'favela', dungarees, rabble – all these words represent human beings – oppressed and exploited people who no longer want others to run their lives, humiliated people who are starting to lift up their heads to see the horizon, people moving towards a different civilization, a new world of genuine fraternity and Christianity.

What one catches here is a vision of a pastor who is prepared to lay down his life for the sheep, who though misunderstood and dubbed 'political' by his superiors, which would include the present Pope, nonetheless is rejoicing in the solidarity he experiences with the oppressed and in the vision he has been shown of their future:

The world we want to make, the new world of brotherhood we hope for, is worth all our sacrifices, and is so magnificent as to give new meaning to everything in our lives. I have accepted the Gospel, and I could not turn back without feeling unworthy. I shall remain, with a clear conscience, at the side of the people, in Rio de Janeiro, in Maranhao, wherever I may be in Brazil, or anywhere else in the world. With a clear conscience, and with the conviction that the Gospel today means achieving agrarian reform, university reform, urban reform, the reform of work-relationships in industry, the struggle against political and economic imperialism and against all forms of oppression. I believe mine is the way of truth, and since it is the nature of truth to diffuse itself, I shall certainly not be able to keep it to myself.[10]

In his wrestling with 'the principalities and powers' of this world, Fr Alipio has not lost anything of his pastoral love for his people: in fact love and hope abound. He knows that faithfulness to Jesus Christ means a fundamental loyalty to the victims of oppression and of injustice. What this revolutionary priest is showing me in his ministry is something essentially basic to the gospel: Jesus did not have to condescend to poor people, to come down to their level, to try and see their problems from their point of view – he was on their level, affected by their poverty, because he was one of them. He was poor. This then constitutes the basic and major challenge to the bishops and the church in England. This process occurs in many parts of the world, where men and women are joyfully taking up the longing of the poor for justice and deliverance from oppression. It has been clear from all the reports that have reached us that the Pope was badly shaken by the cruel poverty of the millions in the favelas, those appalling, hopeless, shanty towns whose inhabitants face a daily battle against hunger and disease. We bishops in Britain are challenged by Archbishop Helder Camara's stirring cri-de-coeur made in New York as far back as 1969 when he took up the cause of the poor.

What ultimately do we want? What are we struggling for? We want to sweep poverty from the face of the earth, poverty which is an insult to the Creator. We want all human beings to be able to realise themselves in such a way that no one is reduced to being an object, a thing: we want all people to see in themselves the image and likeness of the Father, to be in a position to fulfill their profound vocation as co-creators charged by God with dominating nature and completing creation; we want human rights to be a reality.[11]

Who can doubt that we need such bishops in Britain today?

Finally, how shall the church take up the shouts and freedom songs of the oppressed, for it cannot possibly meet the excitement and fervour that the oppressed feel with the type of hymns sung in most Western churches? If freedom is the watchword of the afflicted, it must be a major theme in their hymnody – it only becomes tedious and overplayed when sung in the presence of the exploiting rich and the poor's oppressors. For the struggling poor of Namibia, the taste of freedom is discernible even now in the bread of adversity. The great day of their deliverance needs to be sung out in anticipation of the God who grants deliverance to his saints.

A HYMN TO FREEDOM

Namibia enchained in tyrant's bondage,
Your people plead for freedom to be free
From rod and lash, from terror's sway a hostage,
To you, Lord God, they cry in misery.
How long, O Lord, how long shall evil triumph?
How long, O Lord, shall prisoners captive be?

Help of the helpless, comfort of the mourning,
Hope of the poor, the orphan's sanctuary,
They call for justice, shall that call be heeded?
They cry for mercy, shall they mercy see?
Arise, Lord God of Hosts, their one defender,
Smite tyrants' chains to set your people free.

Arise, Namibia, now your dawn is breaking,
United march to claim your destiny.
A people freed from racist domination,
Reborn in hope, destined for liberty.
Let freedom ring from every hill and valley;
Let justice stream for all the world to see.

To you, Lord God of hosts, be glory given,
You gave us martyrs, give us victory,
The fire of freedom you alone implanted:
Children of freedom may we always be.
Namibia then one nation under heaven,
Upholding justice, truth and equity.

(Sung to the theme of Sibelius' *Finlandia*)

5

The Smile on the Crocodile

Ella Fitzgerald, the great American jazz singer, was being interviewed by a young English woman on one of our TV channels during her week's appearance at a London night-club. Commenting on the black American's popularity, the interviewer, a white, said of pre-war United States theatres, 'Of course, you could not have appeared in them as a black singer at that time.' She was quickly interrupted by the American star who interjected, 'Or here!' The point was well made. White liberals in Britain still cannot concede that racism in all its ugly dimensions exists here. If pressed to admit its existence, they will point to South Africa, or America and say, 'But it's far worse there!' As I write this another 'anonymous' Pakistani has been stabbed to death by four white youths in East London. The black community in these islands is not concerned about comparisons: for them racism not only exists here, it flourishes, it maims, it terrifies large sections of their community and, in fact, is killing some of them. Martin Luther King, on his visit to the United Kingdom to preach in St Paul's cathedral, challenged white complacency over the deterioration in race relations over here when he announced that time had run out for us. White people here, including church members, had a built-in dishonesty when it came to looking facts in the face. There was no racism in Britain, or if there was it was minimal and we could be left to deal with it, as was once said so optimistically about the National Front: 'Ignore them and they will go away.' Dr King had had a more realistic apprenticeship in his struggle for human rights and this allowed him to examine the roots of racism. As far back as 1967 he wrote:

The tragedy of South Africa is not simply in its own policy. It is the fact that the racist government of South Africa is virtually made

71

possible by the economic policies of the United States and Great Britain, two countries which profess to be the moral bastion of the Western world.[1]

Part of the economic life of this country, which was in the past buttressed by its investments and profits from the slave trade, is today still buttressed by its massive investment in a modern form of near slavery, to which Dr King was alluding, that which exists for blacks in South Africa and Namibia. The alliance between British capitalism and the South African government is played down and was an almost hidden conspiracy before the facts were brought before the British public by such groups as Anti-Apartheid, End Loans to Southern Africa, the Namibia Support Committee and others in recent years. Successive British governments have done little or nothing to discourage investment in South Africa by British firms, in fact, British investments have steadily increased there, resulting in British complicity or silence over the atrocities and blatant military adventurism of South Africa in such places as Angola, Namibia, Zimbabwe and Mocambique. Where governments have been acquiescent and ineffective, the churches have been little better.

When I was deported from Namibia in 1972, I was astonished to learn on my arrival back in Britain of the number of churches, including the Church of England (and at least one of her bishops) which had massive investments in South African companies who were exploiting their black labour force. Here indeed was a pretty state of affairs. I had been deported from Namibia after campaigning for fair wages for black workers from companies who were paying large sums of money to churches and fellow Christians in the United Kingdom. Yet churches here condemned groups such as SWAPO, the ANC, PAC, Patriotic Front as organizations which had resorted to arms, but could see little or nothing wrong in investing in apartheid. In fact they appeared angry when a prolonged campaign led by the groups I have mentioned forced many of them, with a fair degree of reluctance, to relinquish the shares they had previously held. In meetings I have addressed in Britain, America, Canada, Belgium, Germany, Holland and Switzerland, the question of investment in South Africa would be the touchiest point – along with the armed struggle – of the whole evening's discussion.

72

What was the cause of this aberration? Western Christians have seen on their television screens such things as the shooting of a thousand children at Soweto, the ceaseless round of student demonstrations and their subsequent dispersal, with sickening violence from the South African police, with the mounting death of demonstrators and innocent by-standers. They may have heard of the atrocities today being committed in Namibia and, from time to time, certain letters of protest will be issued. I never underrate such actions for they are important, as when an archbishop deplores the arrest and detention of someone like Fr David Russell, imprisoned for his defence of the poor squatters at Crossroads in Cape Town. But the accumulated effect of all these protests by heads of churches or the British Council of Churches, significant as they are, is brushed aside by the South African government as flea bites, the mildest form of irritant. So obviously much more is needed. That is not to say that protests should cease, but clearly something more is needed if we wish to be in real and effective solidarity with the oppressed.

In Zurich I attended a meeting with Swiss bankers, held under the auspices of the local council of churches, in which members of the World Council of Churches' Programme to Combat Racism were challenged to defend their policies before members of the local power-ful banking community who were also practising Christians, many of them pillars of their respective churches. If the Swiss 'gnomes of Zurich' were none too charmed with what we were saying and doing in our support of the African freedom movements, I remember that the local clergymen were even more acid and many of their faces belied the expression of Christian goodwill they purported to express to us in their opening speeches of welcome. The main speech of the evening came from a 'Christian' banker, whose father had been a missionary in South Africa 'before Johannesburg was founded', and whose sister was a missionary in Kenya. He deplored what he called the modern trend in religion, the absence of family prayers, grace before meals and Bible reading in the home. He had been taught these things by his father. But today, he said, he abhorred the emphasis on politics which now intruded everywhere, into religion, business, the schools and the universities. He believed, if I recollect correctly, in 'evolution not revolution' and said he was in business to do all he could for his 'black employees'. It was quite a speech, hard hitting against the World Council of Churches, and it brought animated applause from our Swiss hosts, and most particularly from the Swiss clergy present.

In replying I said my father was a businessman. Though not a Christian, he was absolutely honest: he maintained he was in business not for any humanitarian notions but simply to make a profit. If his goods were better or cheaper than anyone else's, he would prosper, if they were not, he wouldn't. But he was forced by British law to pay his workers agreed minimum wages. There was the difference. Swiss firms in South Africa, like British, German, American or Japanese, had unbridled opportunities to make money, a lot of money, because the South African government had the African labour force by the throat. Strikes, or wage bargaining, were eradicated by the most ruthless means, by shootings, tear gas and baton charges. The European investor was in virtual clover. Sixty per cent of South Africa's investment comes from overseas. Three things followed from this in-flow of foreign capital: the South African government was buttressed by a stable economy; the South African workers were being robbed blind and could not effectively resist because of the violent apartheid system paid for from taxes from overseas firms; and those who invested in the system reaped some of the highest profits available anywhere in the world today. Militarism backed by capital investment from abroad were the twin props of the apartheid system.

I concluded my speech by saying that the poor Namibian workers knew who were for them and who were against them and that 'Christian' bankers in Switzerland or anywhere else for that matter, should not try to fool themselves or the world in general. The poor saw them, along with South Africa, as their oppressors. In their struggle to free themselves from South Africa, they were struggling too to free themselves from Western economic exploitation.

Any partial observer at that Zurich meeting could see that there was an easy and happy alliance there between the rich bankers and the church. Many of the former could claim the easiest of relations with the latter: their fathers had been missionaries, church elders, pillars of religion and were accorded respect and admiration by the church both for the positions they held and for their 'philanthropy'. The church in Zurich was clearly at home in the company of the rich, but seemed reluctant to question the morality of how such riches had been

74

attained. What was equally obvious was that the church was not at home with the poor – that is, not with the protesting, articulate, challenging poor. It would probably be true to say the church would be at home with the docile, broken, cringeing, grateful, begging poor who 'knew their place', showed their thanks, and were respectful towards their betters, but they were clearly threatened by the struggling poor such as the freedom fighters, the Soweto students, and other militants in Southern African who challenged their brand of Christianity. As I have said, this is clearly evident to the struggling poor themselves, but why does the church in the West not admit that it is so?

When, for example, poor people in Britain see photographs of the Archbishops of Canterbury and York in clerical evening dress, with court decorations, photographed with a cardinal resplendent in colourful episcopal attire, guests of city businessmen in London, what are they to conclude? They conclude that the church in this country is extremely at ease with the rich and the powerful. Now, I can hear my critics thunder that Jesus dined with publicans and sinners, and so it is not only possible to do this but also laudable. The rich, I am frequently reminded, have souls too. But my critics must admit there are differences. Jesus dined as a poor man, as an open supporter and defender of the cause of the poor and an uncompromising fighter for their rights, and he returned a poor man uncontaminated by the flattery, the blandishments or the compromises the rich exact out of the church. He returned to live with the poor – probably to no home of his own. The style of the rich had not rubbed off on to him. Jesus did not live in a palace: many of our bishops do! He did not dress in fancy clothes: 'they that wear fine raiment are in kings' houses' – should his disciples? His community of faithful believers were not organized on city lines by professional businessmen on salaries of £23,000 per annum.[2] He did say, 'Where your treasure is there will your heart be also.' Is it to be wondered then that the cries of the poor for justice and deliverance will be met by mere tokenism by a church that has set its hearts on earthly treasure?

What would impress the struggling poor if done by bishops and church leaders in this country? Clearly a prophetic crusade would if it were aimed at the religious hypocrisy of such as the rich bankers, the city businessmen and those who today rip off the poor. The signs of this prophetic ministry have been shown among us by such men as the assassinated archbishop, Oscar Romero, of San Salvador, 'who proved he was a great prophet by the things he said and did in the sight of God and of the whole people' (Luke 24.19). Today church manifestoes are clearly not enough: the powerful exploiters of the poor can live in ease with pieces of paper. It is only when the oppressors of the poor are named and the forces of the church are mobilized against them that they in turn show their true nature and attack the church. Actions always speak louder than words. This above anything is what the poor in Britain are waiting for.

I was asked recently to write a foreword to a report on race relations in Britain today called, *Now you do know* by John Downing.[3] I consulted a leading black churchman about what I had written and asked for his comment and criticism. He had nothing with which he was in disagreement, but added, 'You must stress that bishops and others in this country who never bother to read such reports will never again be able to make the excuse – we did not know.' If he is correct, why is it that these leaders do not read such reports, or if they do, that they so seldom take effective action as a consequence? Is it all the fault of the press that when church leaders speak out they rarely make the headlines? I cannot believe it. Yet when are we to get headlines in our newspapers such as 'Archbishop denounces Enoch Powell as Racist', or 'Bishop leads campaign to end loans to South Africa'? But these are political statements, I am told, and are not part of a bishop's or archbishop's responsibility. I am again reminded that they would be a flagrant mixing of religion with politics. But when have archbishops and bishops been deterred from making political statements in this country when the politics have been of the right flavour? Our athletes were told by Mrs Thatcher not to participate in the Moscow Olympics. At least two bishops to my knowledge supported her and went on record to say so. One clear difference between the position of bishops like Romero in San Salvador and those here is this: though he began life as a conservative, in the end he was brought close to the sufferings of society through his close contact with his clergy whom he listened to and respected, and through witnessing the suffering of the poor at close hand. This says something profound about him and his clergy: they were close to the poor, loved the poor, listened to the poor. My own observations of the situation in Britain is that we have here a middle-class church, served by middle-class bishops and priests, most of whom are alienated by culture, life-style and background away from the poor. Certainly exceptions there are, but they are exceptions. The poor are not a priority for the church in England: the rich are!

Of course, there are those who will repudiate this and point to the charitable works of the church with its old people's homes, its orphanages, the work of the Church Army etc. They will also point to the rich who support such 'works of mercy' or 'charity' as contradicting what I am alleging. In Namibia we had similar centres, but their existence never excused the church from demanding justice for the poor and striving for a society in which the need for such institutions would be minimal. The church for too long has been very willing to take conscience money from the rich and has paid an exacting price for so doing – it has sat silent and acquiescent in a society where real justice has evaded the poor. It is the church's dependence on the rich benefactors in this country that has made her content with moderate reform when massive change within her structures and that of surrounding society are called for. If John Browning's book is correct, and I have yet to speak to a member of the black community who would deny it, then mighty actions on behalf of the black oppressed are needed in Britain.

Politicians are quick to point out that they will only act in such situations when they are forced by public opinion to do so. What enormous moral pressure that puts on the church, to act as the conscience of the nation. Those areas where the church's voice should be heard on behalf of the black people in this country are first, the total removal of the SUS laws; second, the abolition of discriminatory immigration laws; third, restraints placed on the police in the acts of aggressive violence committed against both black and white people; and fourth, a demand to end job discrimination. If civilizations are judged on the treatment of their weakest members, then history will certainly condemn our present society in Britain on account of the application of the SUS laws. In other laws a Britisher is regarded innocent until proved guilty. In this instance exactly the reverse is the case; black, and to a limited extent, white youths are considered guilty on the often biased evidence of a policeman that they were thought likely to commit or about to commit a crime. The countless assurances given by leading police commissioners have done nothing to allay the suspicions and hostilities not only of the black community but also of social workers, clergy and others who work closely with black groups. Added to this is the whole concept of police in Britain becoming both apprehender and prosecutor in such cases, something which is unique in Europe, and one can see a situation where injustice abounds.

Britain today has some of the toughest immigration laws in the world. Further, in-coming, would-be immigrants are met with some of the toughest immigration officers too! The virginity tests, the appalling separation of families, the midnight raids on homes and factories, the harassment of the black, particularly Asian members of our society, are more reminiscent of Nazi Germany than of a land which prides itself on its freedom. Freedom for whom, one is bound to ask? The press and television take up, from time to time, the discriminatory practices of the state against those it suspects of violating its immigration laws. (It is high time the church in this country called a halt to such violations as we have seen performed here against black people.)

It is time too that the church acted in the name of mercy to take up the cause of the orphan, the widow and the stranger, as the biblical imperative demands her to do. People fleeing from war in Ethiopia and Eritrea are placed in remand centres for months while their cases are reviewed to see if they are bona fide refugees. The effects of such incarceration on already frightened people can be extremely damaging. Has this country really forgotten how to be merciful? Could not some of our many redundant churches be made over to receive them and could not some of our religious orders and other Christian groups be mobilized to take care of them? 'I was a stranger and you took me in' is still a requisite for those who would enter the kingdom. On this country's present showing, what confidence can we have that we will ever make it?

The diocese of Lincoln has inaugurated a youth training scheme in an attempt to help young unemployed people. But the plight of the black youth in this country and their sense of burning dissatisfaction with the discrimination and other factors that make their unemployment figures nationally higher than those for whites is something that needs tackling. The prophets in Israel were those who took up the cause of the weak and the voiceless at God's behest and made their cause known, promoting it at the cost of their lives. And there lies the rub! When the church takes up the cause of the poor in an effective way, she can be certain that harassment and persecution will automatically follow. The problem then is a personal and theological one. Jesus calls us to lay down our life for his kingdom, but if we are deluded into thinking that Britain is basically a Christian country, that all businessmen, all judges, all policemen, all magistrates and our government always act from such motives then we are of all people the most deluded.

The passion of Jesus shows us a society judged from the point of view of the poorest and the weakest, whose part the Son of Man clearly opted to adopt. Seen from the point of view of the poorest and the weakest, present day British society cannot be treated with the same smug complacent satisfaction in which the rich and powerful view it. Yet Isaiah's demands are just as applicable today as when he made them, 'Cease to do evil, learn to do good, search for justice, help the oppressed, be just to the orphan, plead for the widow' (Isa. 1.17). Britain, like Zion, before her, 'will be redeemed by justice and her penitents by integrity' (Isa. 1.27).

This clearly demands suffering for the church and will provoke both ridicule and anger from those rich people who presently support her. We have had sentiments of this in the reaction of certain members of parliament to the bishops' plea for an investigation into the crises of unemployment facing this country, as well as reaction to the Bishop of Hereford who wishes to use the church's glebe land for permanent residential sites on which to house gypsies. But angry letters and grumblings would be followed by much more threatening behaviour if the church in this country were ever to make an effective stand on behalf of the increasing number of poor here. Our theology clearly teaches us what lies in store for those who follow Christ's way: his end could well be ours. Those who give a cup of cold water in the name of a prophet will receive a prophet's reward: martyrdom! 'For which of the prophets have you not killed?'

The words of the Latin American theologian, Leonardo Boff, are telling:

> The history of human struggle
> for justice and freedom

79

knows few successes.
It is full of martyrs,
defeats,
and long-standing hopes.
It is a history of unrestrained, inexhaustible hope.
The oppressors almost always win the day.
God has guaranteed final victory
in the triumph of the Kingdom of love and goodness,
but God allows the Way of the Cross,
with its suffering and seeming failure,
to go on from one century to the next.[4]

But what can move the church to take up the cause of the oppressed in her midst? She can be appealed to by moving manifestoes such as the following declaration made by certain church leaders in South Africa at Hammanskraal on 11-15 February, 1980, which spoke of the church's role in areas of conflict as follows:

> The Church is the fellowship of those who find their dignity and worth in the forgiving love of God and who seek to live in obedience to Jesus as Lord.
>
> As part of society its members are inextricably involved in the divisions, ambiguities and sins of that society; as part of the Church they belong to a family in which mutual love transcends those divisions. Such love, reflecting as it does the love of Christ, is to be expressed in unequivocal commitment to justice and the oppressed, in mutual care that is ready to reprove and be reproved and endures even when disagreement or the pressures of the world seek to divide. The Church lives in society, sharing its guilt and pain but bearing witness to the judgement of God which condemns the oppressor (Matt. 25.31-46) and his mercy which seeks the lost (Luke 19.10). It endeavours in the power of the Holy Spirit to serve, to suffer and to love in the Name of Christ.[5]

But what ultimately can make her move? Clearly the Holy Spirit working through her prophets, 'Your young men shall see visions and your old men shall dream dreams' (Joel 3.1,2). Where are these seers of visions and these dreamers of dreams? Has God left us without witnesses, has he abandoned his church in the West? When people ask me this I am clearly at a loss to know what to answer: I believe that prophets are there all right, and I have been fortunate in meeting them. The trouble is that the church in this country, like Jerusalem of old, so often rejects them, refuses to hear their message, ignores their witness. I think of Bishop Ambrose Reeves, that stout-hearted crusader for the rights of Africans, shamefully treated by the Church of England, yet having so much to offer it, to inspire it, to contribute to its life, applauded by African leaders with deep love and recognized by world statesmen and the United Nations, yet so badly treated by his own church in England. I think of Trevor Huddleston, Michael Scott, men of outstanding, brilliant talent, yet never fully used by the church at home, respected perhaps, often feared, pointed to when the church needs to defend itself from accusations of being reactionary, yet never given the scope to use their extraordinary gifts to the full. Yet God will continue to raise up prophets 'whether they will hear or whether they will not hear' and not just for England's benefit alone.

Such a one was the outstanding Archbishop of San Salvador, Oscar Romero. I met him briefly at the conference of Latin American bishops in Puebla, Mexico in February 1979. He was assassinated shortly after writing a letter to President Jimmy Carter denouncing United States interference in his country's affairs and especially its military aid to a junta which ruled with savage repression. One of the Archbishop's closest friends, a Jesuit priest, had been murdered by the regime as well as several secular priests. I have chosen Archbishop Romero as a living example of what I believe it means to be a bishop in the modern world. There are those who will dismiss his witness as not being fully applicable to Britain. Things, they will argue, are not nearly as bad here as in El Salvador and there are other voices raised who speak out in this country on behalf of the poor or those with real grievances. The church cannot always be jumping into the public arena stirring things up. It must be sure of its facts, know when to speak and when to refrain. I understand such sentiments and have heard them often enough, but the one special quality about the martyred Archbishop – for I feel he was a martyr – was his close contact with ordinary people, the masses of ordinary workers who exist in every city. They were his driving force, his inspiration if you like, whose cause he upheld and for whom ultimately he died. In every society there are oppressed people and oppressors. The Archbishop made clear his choice. My wish is simply that bishops would do so in Britain today. I believe his witness on behalf of the poor challenges not only bishops but Christians in whatever area they live and work. Let us examine the situation which gave birth to him and tempered his witness. 'The church lives in society, sharing its guilt and pain,' we have said. What is present day society like in El Salvador? This is how CONIP (Coordinadora Nacional de la Iglesia Popular 'Oscar a Romero') describes it:

In El Salvador we are passing through a sad experience of Suffering and Death, which is no more than the culmination of a long history of fifty years of oppression. To be a Christian in our country is a crime for which you pay with torture and death. Our church, which tries to follow its mission of denouncing injustice, is constantly repressed in its pastoral work. In fact the persecution and break-up of the Co-operatives has intensified. The enemies of the people machine-gun the churches and attack church institutions like the Legal Aid Commission of the Archbishopric and its only radio station YSAX. They launch campaigns of opposition and go on to massive round-ups in the most distant cantons and villages. Seven priests have given their lives for justice, the people's cause. They have killed our brave and holy prophet, Mgr Romero, with a bullet through his heart, which was also the heart of the people.

This persecution of Christians is taking place within a broader context of extermination of our people, which is struggling for its liberation from an unjust system which benefits a few and deprives the great majority. Those responsible for maintaining this repressive system imposed on us are the armed forces, the corrupt Christian Democrat ministers and the imperialist government of the United States, which is now preparing a shameless intervention in El Salvador.

The system which actually exists in El Salvador is a system of death and exploitation. Yet 'God does not want the death of his sons, but their conversion and life' (Ez. 18.32). This is why our people – mostly Christian – is organising itself to drive out this detestable system. It is not a matter of importing Revolution; it is a matter of building a new society which responds to our interests and essential characteristics. This will be a society based on Justice and Life for the masses and will be an intervention of the Kingdom

82

of God – which Jesus foretold and exemplified – in history.

Friends, in the name of the thousands of brothers assassinated and persecuted, we are asking humbly, with the anguished voice of a martyred people, for solidarity. In the name of the hundreds of martyrs who perished on the frontier with Honduras, in the name of the murdered priests and our Archbishop Romero, who gave such support to our struggles, we are asking you for MORAL and MATERIAL SOLIDARITY. Help us to meet our enormous commitments, to rescue us from poverty.[6]

I was given an opportunity of discussing the Archbishop's work and idealism with two people from San Salvador, one of whom belonged to a grass roots community there. I have recorded that interview just as it took place in my Peace Centre and believe it will convey the feelings that ordinary people had for him. We will call the two participants Juan and Mariella. This is what they shared with me:

MARIELLA   Archbishop Romero discovered Marxism as an instrument to promote the Christian faith and to change reality. Having made this discovery the Archbishop asked the base communities to have dialogue with him. After his death CONIP came into being. For the masses, the ordinary people, their Archbishop was a symbol. He could express what they could not say. At last the people had a voice to speak for them at a time when all the mass media was closed to organizations representing the people, he spoke out for the ordinary people. Here was a channel of information both to and from the people. People felt great love for him and identified with him because he had identified with them. The main feature of his personality was his utter simplicity. He made no demands on the people. He was there simply to serve them. Everyone knew where he lived. This too was remarkable, for he had chosen to live in a small hospital which cared for people with cancer – in fact, he was shot dead at the altar in the chapel of that hospital saying mass. He would spend Christmas in the shanty towns; New Year also with the poor. He always kept very close to the poor.

COLIN What did the Archbishop mean for you personally?

MARIELLA As a Christian I had always felt guilty in my contact with the church. In the end I did not even have the courage to go to church and read the gospel with other Christians, because I felt rejected as a communist. But when Helder Camara and Archbishop Romero made their voices heard, I felt that there was no inconsistency any longer with holding my position. Before I had felt totally excluded by my fellow Christians. This was a terrible feeling. I went to mass and was shown a faith which was supposed to be lived alone with no contact with other people. For me it was like going to nowhere. It meant having to live a double life – you had to live your political life with people who didn't believe in God, and your Christian life with people who didn't have a political stance. In the end you tried to keep your faith to yourself, but you can't have an individual faith! This struggle in the end alienates Christian people and in the end you lose contact with them. But for me, with the situation in El Salvador, due to the influence of the Archbishop, I discovered to my joy that people can be Marxist and Christian at the same time.

JUAN (speaking about the Archbishop as the ordinary people saw him and his role in Salvadorian society). They felt at last they, the poor, had a father, a pastor, someone who could lead them. When he died they felt alone, not because the Archbishop was a paternalist, but because he had been able to stand up for their rights. That was when they had decided to form CONIP. I remember the Archbishop used to say that in El Salvador God was calling both groups to his reign (kingdom). Previously the authorities in the church thought the church's place was to stay in the middle, but Romero pointed out that when the church is in the middle it is out of history, because history is always written as a fight between the exploited and the exploiters. Since the Christian community in El Salvador could no longer be neutral, it had to take a definite stand against the exploiters. God's kingdom is a kingdom of justice and truth, and reality in El Salvador necessitates that the church breaks into the situation by solving the contradiction. It necessitates destroying one class, not because we hate it, but because it is the only way of making real what God promises, what God asks us to build – oppression must go! We must now organize the people into a revolutionary front. We are confident of achieving our political aims because the people now understand they have to fight. They have been offered so little in the way of reform ...

COLIN And what would the Archbishop think about that?

JUAN There are only two choices open to us in our society, the

Archbishop used to say. The first is the domination of the middle classes which is oppressive to the poor masses of the people. The other is the choice offered by the people themselves. This is what is being fought for by the people. He seemed implicitly to recognize that war was necessary. We had seen with admiration the way his thinking was developing. In his last speech he implored, he begged, the soldiers not to kill the people!

COLIN But would the Archbishop have asked the people not to kill the soldiers?

JUAN He had always taught that killing just for the sake of killing was utterly wrong and he was opposed to it, but he also believed that people had the right to defend themselves. In his position I suppose it was too difficult for him to say anything stronger. The Pope had told Romero to be objective in his criticisms of the regime. The Archbishop had said in a sermon shortly after his discussion with the Pope that he was grateful for what the Pope had said. He re-stated that he always asked God to guide him to where the truth was. He really did try to study reality. He respected the people *and the people changed him* (my italics).

MARIELLA But the middle classes hated him. They thought he had betrayed them so they were angry with him because they felt he was too political.

COLIN Did he die for politics or did he die for the people?

MARIELLA People felt they had lost their father, their true pastor. It wasn't that he went too far, became too political, it was that he was always defending poor people, always speaking out on their behalf. I don't know what the Pope said about him. I remember the Archbishop said the Pope thought he was acting in the right way but that he must be more prudent, more careful.

COLIN What did the church say about him after his death? What was reported about this in El Salvador?

JUAN It was reported that the Vatican regretted his death, because he had become the voice of the people in San Salvador. The Pope also sent a papal nuncio from Mexico to speak at his funeral but before he could give his sermon at the requiem, the military opened fire. After the massacre he made a statement but it was ambiguous. There were other bishops, though, and these spoke out more courageously in his defence.

It has been my experience both in South Africa and Namibia that the state can deal there with fractious priests who speak out against it with a fair degree of confidence and effectiveness when it can contain their protests within the South African context. When such critics arouse the interest and concern of the international community then they have to be severely dealt with. This would be true in the case of Dr Beyers Naude and most recently with Bishop Desmond Tutu. In the case of Archbishop Romero it seems to me certain that his challenging letter to Jimmy Carter precipitated his own death. Readers will judge for themselves how far the Archbishop had travelled. A ministry that begins by defending the rights of the people in the shanties ends by challenging with utter frankness the leader of the world's most powerful nation. I include the whole text in translation of this powerful letter:

Mr President,

A few days ago a piece of news, which caused me serious concern, appeared in the national press. According to it, your government is looking into the possibility of giving financial support as well as military assistance to the present junta.

Because you are a committed Christian and have repeatedly expressed your intention of defending human rights, I take the liberty both of putting my pastoral viewpoint before you and of making a precise demand.

I am seriously concerned by the news that the government of the United States is studying ways of accelerating the arms race in El Salvador, by sending teams of military advisers 'to train three battalions from El Salvador in logistics, communications and intelligence'. If this true, your government, far from contributing to a more just and peaceful society, will, on the contrary, be supporting injustice and the repression of an organized people which has often fought for its most basic human rights. The present junta and above all the armed forces and security services have, unfortunately, never given proof of their ability to solve, both in the short and the long term, the serious problems which face the nation.

They have, on the whole, resorted to repressive violence, which has resulted in a number of dead and wounded far greater than under the previous regimes whose systematic violation of human rights was denounced by the Pan-American commission on human rights of the OEA.

The brutal manner in which the security forces expelled the leaders of the Christian Democrats by eliminating some of them, and this it would appear without the permission of the government or the party, this brutality clearly shows that the junta and the Christian Democrats do not rule the country; power is in the hands of the unscrupulous military who only know how to repress the people and support the ruling class.

If it is true that last November 'a group of six Americans were in El Salvador delivering and demonstrating $200,000 worth of gas masks and bullet-proof jackets', then you should know that since then the security forces, thus protected, have been able to repress the masses both more effectively and more violently, thanks to the use of lethal weapons.

Also as a citizen of El Salvador as well as its Archbishop, I have to try and make sure that both Christianity and justice reign in our country. That is why, if you really do want to defend human rights I ask you:

– stop all military aid to the government of El Salvador.
– give us a guarantee that your government will not seek, by whatever means, whether military, economic, diplomatic, etc. to oppose the wishes of the people of El Salvador.

At the present time our country is experiencing a serious economic as well as political crisis. It cannot be doubted that the people are more politically aware and better organized. They are, therefore, more responsible and more able to govern El Salvador; they alone are capable of resolving the crisis.

It would be unjust and unfortunate if, thanks to the intervention of other countries, the people of El Salvador were frustrated, repressed and unable to decide for themselves the economic and political path our country should follow. It would violate a right which was recognized by the conference of Latin American priests in Puebla: 'the legitimate self-determination of the people of Latin America which entitles them to organize themselves in accordance with their traditions and their history and to help in the establishment of a new international order'.

87

I sincerely hope that your religious feelings and your wish to defend human rights will allow you to agree to my demand, in order that more blood should not be shed in our long-suffering country.

With my greetings,
Oscar A. Romero – Archbishop. [7]

My own tribute to the martyred Archbishop was written in the form of this poem:

ARCHBISHOP ROMERO

Today
Good Friday
fell like a stone
With it came
a death rattle from
a tomb called
San Salvador
Blinding
darkness spread
silent as a
muffled scream from
Golgotha's
moaning hill
as peasant women
choked and suffocated
under the piled up
bodies of their
dead crushed
children
innocent guests
at a gun
toting funeral

where they
were given a
special one only
panoramic
performance a
world premiere
laid on by shy
grinning dictators
who hide their
midget minds
behind
dark glasses
The funeral
obsequies were
sung to that
old familiar
Latin American
beat of flying
glass and
exploding hand
grenades as
snipers from

the mourning
police militia
flicking away
an occasional
tear gas tear
shot up
in self defence
unarmed
women children
and ever
ready
students
communists all to
the last unsuspecting
corpse
They display
not the calm
satisfaction
of a job well
done manifesting
to a stunned
world their total

faith hope and
perjury
in their golden
dollar brand
republic   Death
knew no religious
scruple and a
power was on
parade which
spelt out in
cantons of
cannon fire
their litany for
a dying
god   The heap
of cheap
sandals shoes
of the fallen
tank crushed
bomb blasted
poor lay silent
momentos that here
was holy
blood purchased
ground and there
the dead Christ

figure their Jesus
gunned down beside
a chapel
altar   One only
one bullet was
all it took from
a Judas aimed
custom built all
American gun
for all seasons
fired precisely
according to
maker's instructions
clean
    neat
        no fuss
and no expensive
state investigations
that unnecessarily
use up money
needed to construct
air conditioned
torture
chambers   Colonels
generals
paid assassin

all registered pain
shocked disbelief
and dried their
eyes on medals
polished at the
ready for the
death deodorised
requiem of a
whole epoch
Friends
rest easy tonight
democracy has
once again been
proudly preserved
whole in El
Salvador
A nation
died that day
alone
with its archbishop
and waits now
clothed in blood
soaked in grave
clothes
for resurrection.

6

The Sign of Hope

We begin this chapter with a question: What does the church mean for you? For a crushing ninety per cent of our fellow countrymen the immediate answer is an obvious one. They would reply quite frankly, 'Nothing!' Church for them would be the building at the bottom of the road. It might evoke memories of community hymn singing on Sunday night's TV or the parson in the tweed jacket with the pipe maybe, harmless, well-intentioned, but little more. It could also be associated with the annual Christian Aid envelope stuffed under the door that they lose, ignore or angrily declaim against with such words as, 'We've got too many of 'em alive in this country without sending money to keep 'em alive in Africa!' (Christian Aid collectors, incidentally, have also been encouraged to 'atom bomb' the lot!) The church is used less and less for baptisms, funerals and weddings. One outstanding East End bishop speaking lovingly of his flock said, 'They'll do anything for me except go to church.'

Church statistics in this country make for sober reading and like most figures can be interpreted to say almost anything. What these figures tell me is the vast majority of people in this country owe no allegiance to the churches. Yet a slight increase in, for example, the figures for confirmations in a given year or the numbers taking holy communion will be a source of euphoric joy for certain harassed church dignitaries. They react to a small percentage increase much as young girls react to horoscopes. Using business language, they will talk in such terms as 'coming through the depression'. Others will use such expressions as 'we are still basically a Christian country' without either defining how they come to this conclusion or what is meant by it. If pressed and asked, for example, what the Christian attitude was

91

on war, cruise missiles, racism, unemployment, they would admit there is no one Christian position, but that Christians would be just as divided as the rest of society. Others would declaim that these are not subjects with which the church should be involved. What then does give Christians their distinct characteristic? The majority of Christians would answer, their belief in and membership of the church. Like the early Christian writer they would perhaps answer,

> The wealthy among us help the needy; and we always keep together; and for all things wherewith we are supplied we bless the Maker of all through His Son Jesus Christ, and through the Holy Spirit. And on the day called Sunday, all who live in cities or in country places gather together to one place, and the memoirs of the apostles or the writings of the prophets are read, as long as time permits; then, when the reader has ceased, the president verbally instructs, and exhorts to the imitation of these good things. Then we all rise together and pray, and when our prayer is ended, bread and wine and water are brought, and the president in like manner offers prayers and thanksgivings, according to his ability, and the people assent, saying the Amen; and there is a distribution to each, and a participation of that over which thanks have been given, and to those who are absent a portion is sent by the deacons. And they who are well-to-do, and willing, give what each thinks fit; and what is collected is deposited with the president, who succours the orphans and widows, and those who, through sickness or any other cause, are in want, and those who are in bonds, and the strangers sojourning among us, and in a word takes care of all who are in need.[1]

Most Christians in Britain realize that many of the things the Christian church used to provide have been taken over by secular society which can often do them as well, sometimes even better. I travel a lot and I am always amazed at the speed with which I am welcomed and made to feel at home in Christian communities around the world, whether in a sophisticated area of Bonn or on an Indian reservation in Canada. But I am sure that members of Rotary, Round Table, or even the National Front could say the same: hospitality, friendship, sharing are not things which are unique to the church. Worship was once held to be the unifying factor which bound Christians together, but that no longer need be the case. The massive uniformity of the Roman mass swept away since Vatican II is now replaced throughout the world by a myriad of different services, which though basically the mass, are now performed according to different cultural patterns. The mass which once united Roman Catholics is now a source of contention in many parts of Europe, as witnessed by the enormous fuss and commotion caused by the geriatric Archbishop Lefebvre who still clings to a Latin mass and can usually count on a hundred or two equally geriatric-minded congregants panting after the days of wine and roses, when the mass was surrounded by mystery and the laity's job was to 'assist' at it while the priest mumbled on with the interminable Latin mumbo-jumbo. The wind of change is blowing throughout Christendom, which some find terrifying, but others welcome as clearing away the accumulated dross that tarnishes the current image of the church in our present society. There are still those who, amazingly enough, want Christianity to be a sort of mystery religion, crammed to overflowing with miracles, wonder works, supernatural happenings more suitable to the circus tent than the Christian faith. These things have been around with us for centuries and in certain places are a long time dying. Given the uncertainty of our present age and the upheavals caused by the economic chaos that now assaults our society, the danger of turning religion into an occult, a series of processing madonnas, attended by gorgeously robed clerics will become more and more attractive to those in our society who are looking to the church to provide a haven from life's storms, a rock to cling to or an ark to hide in. Though it is not for me to scorn the religious expressions of poor people, yet, nevertheless, I cannot see in the cult of middle-class Mariology the hope for the future of the church in this country.

I know this will draw howls of protest from archbishops to altar boys who will tell me that anything that succeeds in getting people to say their prayers, which draws solid and sincere masses of Christians together, which emphasizes the spiritual in the midst of one of the most secular societies in the world, cannot be dismissed so lightly. 'Take Walsingham away with its large processions of hymn singing and praying people and what are you left with?' they will ask me. 'And now it is for my hope . . . that I am on trial' (Acts 26.6), Luke has Paul saying in his speech before King Agrippa and I can be challenged too. What is the hope that is in me? The challenge tells me as much about my contemporary fellow Christians in Britain as my answer will tell me about me. I sense a sort of desperation to be assured that things are not really as bad with the church as we instinctively feel or think and that we do still count for something to some people and are or can be an influence for good on contemporary society. When I address meetings of clergy, students, congregations at worship on Sunday, or the local sessions of deanery synods, I am struck by one factor: many people are aware that there are deep problems, they wish the church would or could get to grips with them, but experience a deep sense of frustration, sometimes alienation with the whole system, as the following letter to *The Times* newspaper on 1 August 1980 clearly shows:

Sir,

As a member of the General Synod I hope the appointment of Mr Owen, QC, as Dean of the Arches (report, July 30) will encourage the dismantling of the archaic, vexatious and expensive legal substructure with which the Church of England is at present burdened.

Over a period of years resentment has built up in the Synod – not against the legal officers themselves, but at the failure of the church at the centre to initiate any substantial law reform.

No doubt the civil anomalies of the Act of Settlement are just as vexatious to the Crown as the payment of a fee of £150 by the Church of England for the resignation of a Suffragan Bishop is to the ordinary churchgoer.

Are canonical oaths of obedience taken as a deacon and again as a priest really necessary? Are we really justified in asking the people in the pews to produce more and more money when so much is frittered away on non-essential purposes?

It seems to me this is exactly the same syndrome which exists in the political world too. They are desperately looking for messiahs but mediocrity abounds. Even the press has this deep gut reaction and revels in building up the mass appeal of the Pope and the Queen Mother in order to fill the gap which exists in our present society. Is it that we are not producing great people any more in the West, or that a cynical news media smashes our potential idols before they can take on god-like dimensions?

In the Namibian struggle death, torture, imprisonment, cruel unjust sufferings destroy fine young people full of idealism as well as claiming the lives of old people and little children too. The shock waves that assault one repeatedly from Namibia are similar to what was experienced in Britain during the war. In the 1940s we lived with death, saw it claim the lives of teenage pilots as well as children bombed in the tubes and in industrial tenements. As a nation there were times when we were in a state of shock: black people in Namibia share that same experience today. In that way there were times of false hope and times of real hope and with hindsight perhaps we have learnt to distinguish between what was false and what was true. Today when people feel they are 'just living and partly living' it would be extremely dangerous as well as dishonest to paint a euphoric picture about the state of the church in Britain or Christianity in general here to say there was hope when it was otherwise. Few can doubt that the church in this country cries out for reform, renewal, rebirth. Do we beg the question when we say this is the work of the Holy Spirit, passing the buck as if to say 'Well, God can do wonders, so perhaps he has got a miracle or two tucked away in his sleeve'? Now because the Holy Spirit works through people, the ultimate answer to the question, 'Can these bones live?' (Ezek. 37.3) is an unqualified 'Yes', because the Spirit of the living God has the power to bring new life 'to those who live in darkness' and (therefore) 'in the shadow of death', those 'living and partly living' Christians. How? The text in Ezekiel tells us that it was the voice of prophecy which raised them to life again, and that this voice was hope-filled, offering them a new life in a restored homeland. The burden of the message is that God takes people out of the graves they have dug for themselves, from the doom-filled sense of failure that leads to moral paralysis, to cynical hope-less, joy-less lives. The power is there, is it not the prophecy which is lacking?

I prophesied as he had ordered me, and the breath entered them; they came to life again and stood up on their feet, a great, an immense army.
    Then he said, 'Son of Man, these bones are the whole house of Israel. They keep saying: "Our bones are dried up, our hope has gone; we are as good as dead" ' (Ezek. 37.10-12).

95

The order is clear cut: 'So prophesy.' Easier said than done! Here is the problem; 'A voice commands; "Cry!" and I answered, "What shall I cry?" – "All flesh is grass . . . The grass withers, the flower fades . . ." '(Isa. 40.6,7), but that is never the total picture. Hope always rests in the power of the living God to fulfil what he, in his justice, has ordained and so 'the word of God remains for ever' (Isa. 40.8).

We may well ask what was it that muted prophecy, prevented it from speaking out for the living God and diverted it into being the pliant tool that the false prophets made of it? This happened when it was used in the service of an erring, corrupt monarchy, when it was used to soothe the flabby consciences of the rich. When the prophet thus abandons the service of the Lord who demands righteousness, his prophecy collapses; it is a hollow sham. The glory of the true prophet is that he is a mouthpiece of the God who demands justice for the poor, the widow, the orphan and the stranger in the midst. The blindness of the Pharisees was that they attempted to substitute religious rituals in the place of justice and mercy. Are we not guilty of the same in our Western churches today? God humbled Israel through exile. Is not a great 'humbling' needed so that the church in the West shall rediscover the prophetic role that awaits it when it takes up the cause of the poor and the oppressed with the same total commitment to them as did its Lord? But is this gross sentimentality? The world being what it is, Britain being what it is, how can the church abandon those who provide it with its financial support?

The obvious answer is that without the force, the impelling strength of the Holy Spirit, it will not and cannot. It will go on serving the rich and remain at peace with them. But am I wrong in believing that, as the poor in this country are made, more and more, to carry the burdens and suffer the deprivation of present economic policies, that their sufferings and general plight will either compel more Christian leaders to take up their cause, or will polarize them even further from the poor than is the case at present? Am I being over-dramatic in suggesting that the challenge of the poor in our midst is there and, if the voice of prophecy is not raised, it is because our spiritual leaders are not among the poor as being one with them as the prophet Ezekiel was among them, in the sense that is conveyed by the opening sentence of his book: '. . . as I was *among* the exiles on the bank of the river Chebar, heaven opened and I saw visions from God' (Ezek. 1.1).

What are we asking of the leaders of the church? That they become open to the needs of the poor and to their challenge to us to simplify our way of living, to take up their cause against the rich and those who oppress them, no longer to remain silent as the poor struggle to discover their true humanity, denied them in an age which puts profit before the needs of human beings. It is high time for the church's spiritual leaders in this country to opt solidly for the poor and to be seen to be doing so. The hope is there all right: it was when the prophet was *among* the exiles, in the midst of their sufferings, surrounded by their utter sense of hopelessness, and sharing with them in their deprivations, was at one with them, that heaven opened and he saw visions from God. The same Spirit propels Jesus to the downtrodden, those whom society enchains, the struggling poor. Jesus' option must be that of his church today.

Biblical hope is not to be seen as a chirpy, cheery, unrealistic optimism: but it is something which is offered to us through the resurrection of Christ 'so that we, now we have found safety, should have a strong encouragement to take a firm grip on the hope that is held out to us. Here we have an anchor for our soul, as sure as it is firm, and reaching right through beyond the veil' (Heb. 6.18,19).

So where is there this strong encouragement for me to take a firm grip on hope? The Epistle places this hope firmly in God acting through Jesus, he who in the power of God triumphed over every evil men flung at him. He is the hope: it is he who sustains us in our struggle for the achievement of justice and liberation. 'Let us not lose sight of Jesus, who leads us in our faith and brings it to perfection' (Heb. 12.2).

The ever-living hope for the Christian is that Jesus is incarnate, actually in our midst in the poor. The resurrection perpetuates this presence of Christ in our midst in the person of poor people. Each human being reminds us of Christ who was incarnate, and 'lived among us' (John 1.14). God's preference, as shown in the birth of his son as a poor child into a poor family, clearly was for the poor. In serving, loving, and dying for them, the church is imitating her master. Humanity has been described as the 'greatest manifestation of God in our world'. Much of the joylessness, so often a characteristic of Western religion, is self-inflicted and may be traced to the absence of the poor from our midst. Further, the joy which the writer

97

of the Epistle to the Hebrews ascribes to Jesus, even as he faced death, is known by those who take up the cause of the poor. 'Happy (are) those who are persecuted in the cause of right' (Matt. 5.10) is no idealistic piece of sloganeering: those who have known the love, the deep privilege of sharing with the poor in their struggle against their oppressors already experience the 'blessedness' of which Jesus speaks. Hope abounds in the midst of the struggling poor, for they are Christ resurrected in our world. To abandon them is to abandon him; to deny them is to deny him. Their songs of freedom have power to inspire and uplift one in the same way as do some of our most cherished Christian hymns, for one has been able to see the proof of their commitment in the courage of their lives sacrificed to obtain a finer and juster world. As the spirit of Jesus lived on and inspired the apostles under flogging and hardships to sing hymns in captivity, so that same spirit inflames the lives of countless people struggling to obtain the new creation. I meet them daily in my work and during my travels. They are people like Emmanuel, a poor peasant returning to Ecuador to help organize university students there to work for a new, more just society: this means revolution and he is prepared to face death by torture to achieve it. There is Martha, quietly working to find homes for the children of Chilean political prisoners who were killed in the gaols of the junta or 'disappeared' without trace. The gentleness and love that surrounds her speaks of the inner peace she has achieved as a Christian and a socialist. There are the four Zimbabwean students who also have found something to lay down their lives for – the building of a nation freed from the destructiveness of racism. There is Festus, an African priest, ready to face imprisonment and certain torture in Namibia rather than compromise his Christian beliefs in the dignity and worth of each black person. 'With so many witnesses in a great cloud on every side of us' (Heb. 12.1) we have to 'keep running steadily in the race,' the author of the Epistle declares. 'Running', not idling, stagnating, dawdling: the word betokens action, commitment, dedication to the cause. Where does one find such Christian athletes who can inspire us with this living hope?

Well, strangely enough I begin with one who, though dedicated to the Christian faith, said that she personally could see no hope within the church as it is presently constituted in Britain. Without disclosing her identity, I would wish to say that she has inspired and guided me with penetrating honesty and kindly advice for several years. I have come away from meetings with her absolutely determined to struggle on when I had reached breaking point. Yet when I asked her to tell me what hope she saw for the church in Britain this was her reply, 'I have no hope!' Is this the sin of despair then? I think not: it seems to me to have more the ring of prophetic analysis. She referred me to Archbishop William Temple's *Readings in St John's Gospel*, chapter sixteen, in which he says:

> When we pray 'Come, Holy Ghost, our souls inspire', we had better know what we are about. He will not carry us to easy triumphs and gratifying successes; more probably He will set us to some task for God in the full intention that we shall fail, so that others, learning wisdom by our failure, may carry the good cause forward. He may take us through loneliness, desertion by friends, apparent desertion even by God; that was the way Christ went to the Father. [2]

I interpret this in several ways, one of which is as follows: My dearest wish is the liberation of Namibia, for whose freedom I am quite prepared to give my life. I am conscious that I may never see the fulfilment of this hope within my own lifetime. I am more conscious of the many, many failures to achieve or accomplish what I might have achieved, as well as my failures to convince people, to win over support for our struggle within this country and elsewhere. I am deeply conscious of my failures to love, to show more patience when people have shown an inability to grasp our situation or have responded with stubborn aggression or anger. My constant reproach to myself is, if I had been more loving, perhaps Bishop X would have responded or Archbishop Y might have been more positive. But the very failing has its lessons to teach to my brother and sister Namibians who will come after me and who will carry forward the struggle, learning from my mistakes. God can use my failures as well as my successes. This is a cause for great hope, 'When I am weakest then am I strongest!' God can turn my failures into triumphs: this is the mystery of the Cross.

My next source of hope does not spring from within the church itself, but is gleaned from those outside the church whose example and commitment in their struggle for freedom has continued to inspire me. Exile has left many scars but it has also had its moments of blessing. To experience 'the church beyond the church,' the church outside the church, has been one of my happiest discoveries. To be liberated from the 'them and us syndrome' of Christian particularism is a wonderful deliverance indeed. To see clearly that God has given us many partners from different backgrounds for us to work with in close harmony as real brothers and sisters has been one of the real joys of the past eight years of exile. I think I had always recognized the real goodness and worth of people of different faiths or none, but perhaps I did it in a somewhat condescending way. Today I see them in a new light. I have come to know shop stewards, workers from different industries, atheists, campaigners for nuclear disarmament, teachers, TV personalities, lecturers, professors, who in their own way are trying valiantly to make this world a better and more decent place in which to live. They have shared their dreams with me and I have caught the inspiration behind their struggles and have come away from such meetings humbled and strengthened. I have been conscious that many of them, though unable to express 'orthodox' virtues or support credal statements about God, have a commitment to justice beyond that of the majority of those of us who call ourselves Christians. They are those of whom Jesus said, 'Anyone who is not against us is for us' (Mark 9.40). I appreciate with a real sense of joy that these too in a very deep and meaningful way are my real brothers and sisters. I would never say to them, 'You really are a Christian, you know, if you would only admit it.' My joy proceeds from the knowledge of what happened to me: that the scales of myopia have been removed from my eyes by the God who has given me such fellow-workers who, by their deeds and commitment, desire a world where peace, sharing, true sisterhood and brotherhood can abound. They have opted for the cause of love, which is the cause of Christ. The sentiment is better described in a fuller, much wider context by the late Thomas Merton, who had by the time of his death broken out from a Christian strait-jacket and had found deep loving friendships with such men as the Dalai Lama with whom he had profound discussions on prayer. I quote Merton here because of the power of the love that gripped him and the need for such love to possess what is so often our love-starved church in the West. This is what Merton wrote:

In Louisville, at the corner of Fourth Avenue and Walnut Street, in the centre of the shopping district, I was suddenly overwhelmed with the realization that I loved all these people, that they were mine and I theirs, that we could not be alien to one another even though we were total strangers. It was like waking from a dream of separateness, of spurious self-isolation in a special world, the world of renunciation and supposed holiness. The whole illusion of a separate holy existence is a dream. Not that I question the reality of my vocations, or of my monastic life: but the conception of 'separation from the world' that we have in the monastery too easily presents itself as a complete illusion: the illusion that by making vows we become a different species of being, pseudo-angels, 'spiritual men', men of interior life, what have you.

Certainly these traditional values are very real, but their reality is not of an order outside everyday existence in a contingent world, nor does it entitle one to despise the secular: though 'out of the world' we are in the same world as everybody else, the world of the bomb, the world of race hatred, the world of technology, the world of mass media, big business, revolution, and all the rest. We take a different attitude to all these things, for we belong to God. Yet so does everybody else belong to God. We just happen to be conscious of it and to make a profession out of this consciousness. But does that entitle us to consider ourselves different, or even better than others? The whole idea is preposterous.

This sense of liberation from an illusory difference was such a relief and joy to me that I almost laughed out loud. And I suppose my happiness could have taken form in the words: 'Thank God, thank God that I *am* like other men, that I am only a man among others.'

I too thank God I am just a man among other men and women.

Matthew, in the opening chapter of his gospel, shows a world waiting and questioning, 'Where is the infant king of the Jews?' (Matt. 2.2). Like them, we are waiting and searching too. We are looking and yearning for a truly liberated church but are we right to look for a liberating movement from the top? Will the church – Anglican, Roman Catholic, Orthodox, Protestant – be reformed from above? Not even Pope John could achieve that. Certainly he could initiate and set in motion the Council, but once that was done it was the work of God's Holy Spirit to motivate, inspire others to continue the work once conceived by the pontiff. The Council itself was startled, considerably so by the input of the bishops from the so-called Third World, both by the forthrightness of their speeches and by their commitment to the poor. Bishops from the rich Western churches sat silent as these 'spirit filled' spokesmen of the poor challenged the church to change or die, and called on them to make their option for the poor of this world. Today, we see the Roman Church as the most reformed branch of Christendom, but having said that, we know that the process of reform needs to be on-going – too many scars still mar her as well as other churches. 'The wind blows wherever it pleases' (John 3.8), Jesus tells Nicodemus, and you cannot tell 'where it is going'. Once unleashed the power of the Spirit is endless. It took enormous courage for an aged Pope even to conceive of a Council let alone call one into being, but the whole of Christendom has been affected by what he set in motion. Reform in the church cannot be achieved through a tinkering do-it-yourself approach: it presupposes a passionate commitment, a dedication to truth. 'I give my life for the council', were the Pope's dying words and were typical both of the man and the commitment. Men like Pope John are rare indeed, perhaps one to an epoch, so does that mean that the Holy Spirit is thwarted and that without such dynamic leadership the church must flounder? Like the Baptist before him, 'John was a lamp alight and shining and for a time you were content to enjoy the light that he gave' (John 5.35). But we are surrounded by lights, the trouble is we so often look in the wrong direction to catch their brilliance. It is true they do not shine out too often from the palaces of bishops or high ecclesiastics, but God has not left himself without his witnesses. We will not pick them up, though, with easily identifiable tabs on them, as we do articles in the supermarket, marked Methodist, Anglican, Catholic, or in God's service. 'He touches all, especially those who by their lives struggle for what Jesus himself struggled and died for, even though they do not make explicit reference to him and to his universal salvic meaning,'[4] is how Boff puts it. And the poet Lisandero de la Torre in describing 'The Generation of the '30s' speaks of these *lights* as follows:

they attacked minions, they signed manifestoes
and went to jail
to endure the lice that were bequeathed to them.
They did not lose their sense of humour
even though the thing was not a joking matter.
And amid jokes, quixotic acts and fantasies,
with turmoil and commotion as a backdrop,
blending nostalgia and courage
they surrendered to the Great Midwife of History.
They died with lungs undone by tuberculosis,
kicked to death,
shot in the streets,
murdered while they slept,
fighting in the trenches of defeated revolutions.
They tried to change life
because they loved it too much.[5]

Would we recognize these 'heroes' who struggled and died believing they were giving their lives for a better world, whose creation always seemed to evade them? In the same way did people recognize those whom the author of the Epistle to the Hebrews extols in his famous chapter 11, those who were stoned, beheaded, sawn in half, penniless, given nothing but ill-treatment, the weak people who were given strength to be brave in war, those who submitted to torture, those who refused to be released from prison, 'so that they would rise to a better life'. I meet their modern contemporaries daily as they come to visit my community at our Peace Centre, or ask us to take part in some organized, unheralded act of solidarity. The world and the church mostly ignore them, but they exist all right and shine for me as lights of the freedom they yearn to secure for the suffering masses they represent. Let us name just a few of them: they are the exiled students from Soweto planning a memorial service for Steve Biko and trying to rally support from a none-too-concerned London Christian community. They are the Indian journalist fighting to expose the cruelties of the immigration laws and the devastating effect they have on her people in the United Kingdom. They are the peasant from Uruguay who wants help to organize the first meeting of scattered

103

exiles and turns to the church for assistance. They are the Bengali youth who describes the brutality of the British police against members of his own community and has dedicated his life to organizing his people to resist. And they are the British worker battling with life on a modern council house estate and as a shop steward struggling to obtain a fair deal for the labour force in a local factory. We can call him Ray. To say I am wildly excited by his commitment is a gross understatement, but more than that, I see his very existence as one of the new shoots of the Spirit, a sign of hope, a light for those who are able to see it. This is his story as told by himself:

... I became conscious of being a follower of Jesus about the age of fourteen years, which was about the same time that I became interested in Socialism. From the start I have found much in the Bible, Socialism, Jesus, Marx, that is an expression of common aims, such as brother and sisterhood, social justice, liberation from oppression, good news for the weak and poor, social morality and so forth. Also, Christianity and Socialism share similarities in their historical development in that there has often been a disparity, 'a credibility gap', between ideals and reality, teaching and practice. Stalinism and state capitalism are to Socialism what the church and state religion are to Christianity. As Russia turned away from Internationalism under pressure from Western capitalism, so the church has turned in on itself under pressure from social changes it opposed and failed to understand. The inspiring concepts of Internationalism and Catholicism have been given over to beliefs in elites and elects. Yet from Christianity and Socialism for me come the most exciting and inspiring concepts and developments of human society. While Christianity and Socialism share a great deal in common, they also have unique elements that each desperately needs to balance the other. Our faith calls us to love God, yet how is it possible to love God outside of loving our fellow man. Socialism provides the mechanism for turning the sentiment 'love' into a social reality. The social morality of Christianity often makes us aware of injustice, but without the mechanism to act we become, at worst sympathetic or pathetic bystanders, and at best social ambulancemen, manning soup queues, but unable or unwilling to prevent them forming.

My experiences of Socialism and the church have, however, been very different. First, with all the usual personal and structural problems of human organization, I have found the socialist society a meaningful, welcoming body of people, deeply concerned with the quality of life for others in the community, being both aware of needs and prepared to work and fight to achieve them. Prepared to accept and involve on the basis of commitment and willingness to share, outside my family, this community provides me with my support, companionship and motivation.

My early experience of the church was rather different. It was a form filling, profile keeping, register signing world, dotted with half-rimmed spectacled aged academic anachronisms, who appeared to believe that a 'conference' was the immediate response and partial cure to the 'problems of life', and the more pained the title or the wording of the agenda, the more it was possible to achieve. It was a blind alley into which people charged to escape the world.

To the left were the evangelicals, to whom it would seem that the cure for life is the 'saving of souls', which appears to amount to an introverted trance like state of benign neutrality. Eyes fixed on heaven, they encountered life only when they tripped over it. Replacing the organ with the guitar, the stiff shirt with mental straight jacket, continued membership depended on remembering to punctuate conversations with such pass words as 'alleluia' and 'Praise the Lord', and periodically losing control of one's emotions.

To the right the conservatives, safe behind a barricade of books, Sunday hats, who beat out the leftee flames of the social gospel with rolled up copies of *The Daily Telegraph*. Armed to the teeth with middle-class morality, 'O' levels and the Queen, life was a campaign against pornography and a preparation for the fete. For them the devil was alive and well and living in Moscow.

Ahead loomed the parish, where inspiration led to action, which took the form of cutting the vicarage lawn, raising more money for church items, painting the church, going to church, fetes and jumble sales and so forth. It was during this two year period that my wife Patricia developed from such distractions from life the serum which she eventually used to effectively innoculate herself from religion permanently.

105

Ministry in the church, I was told, was based on the Christian family, which meant the parish, which meant cutting the grass, which left me out, so I escaped under the wire and placed the discomfort experienced down to growing pains while my wife put it down to too much gardening. Various attempts were made to relocate me to the fold. Somehow I managed to keep one pace ahead, and was eventually given up for lost and finally was officially reported *'missing believed lapsed'*. Unlike Patricia, my lapse, far from proving terminal, gave me room to think, and my experiences of working in a factory, college and the Labour Movement, encouraged and deepened my belief in God, and increased the value I placed on the example and life of this incredible revolutionary figure, Jesus. My belief was and is, in a God not of magic and superstition, but of the creator of this world, a real world of knocks and bumps, ups and downs, laughter and tears. A world in which some people rose to great heights, while others fell under buses. It was a world not only of sin to be shunned, but to be experienced, enjoyed, involved in and at times to battle against. I came to believe that people were basically good not evil, and although human history included numerous 'falls' so too it was a history of magnificent courage and outstanding achievement. Corruption in the social structure, poverty, ignorance, oppression etc., are the things that corrupt people, and salvation is the liberation from injustice through the pursuit of the 'kingdom of God', on earth. I have felt a calling to the ministry since my teens and am intent on working this through into practice. My friends and workmates, the Union both inside and outside work, and my friends in the Labour Movement (Labour Party, Communist Party, SWP) all know what I am doing and most of them have given me great encouragement over this year. I have been encouraged by the example and support of various Christian Socialists. Shift work has disjointed my attendance on MTS and attendance at Sunday Branch Meetings of my Union and Labour Party have reduced my contact with the local church to a minimum. This is where I stand, I want the church to recognize what I am doing and to give me enough room to continue to work out my ministry in this area. My early experiences have made me distrustful and suspicious of the church and through that, of you.

In an article in *The Times* entitled 'Attractions and dangers of "house churches" and possession', the newspaper's religious affairs correspondent drew his readers' attention to what he considers to be a 'dangerously unhealthy tendency' in Britain. He writes: 'Of 20 patients admitted to a psychiatric hospital claiming to be possessed by the devil or evil spirits, a high proportion had been in recent contact with charismatic prayer groups and a number had had it suggested to them that they might be possessed ... The phenomenon appears to be associated with the mushrooming of "house groups" or "house churches", of which there may be several thousand in Britain, and which consist of groups of people meeting regularly to engage in unstructured forms of prayer and spiritual experience ... In the cases known (to the doctor), many had a curious blend of what he called half-belief, either apparently making up their own religion, or collecting "an incredible array of bits and pieces from many religions and cults", or claiming to practise Christian prayer while also experimenting with Ouija boards.' It is suggested by one doctor in the article that whereas 'in some cultures it may be women or traditional warriors who find themselves insecure and powerless ... with the decline of religion and the imminence of rapid technological change, it may be the clergy and certain sections of the lower professional and middle classes who are most vulnerable' and have been attracted to such groups experimenting in spiritual healing, exorcism and demonic matters. The article goes on to say, 'Others see the house group movement as potentially or actually harmful ... Many cases are known, and not just Evangelical, where the setting up of a charismatic group has begun a period of tension and quarrelling in a local congregation.'[6]

Of course there are house churches and house churches and Clifford Longley does well to point out the dangers of introverted groups dabbling in psychic phenomena. There is, however, a strong movement through the world of Christian grassroots communities who deserve detailed study because they have much to share with Christians in Britain, are involved in important local and national issues and do not produce the introverted, psychologically unstable person that Longley refers to in his article. On the contrary, they are composed of mature Christians, who together with their contemporaries, are seeking through frank and open discussion to apply biblical truths to the major problems of contemporary society. Unlike their Western counterparts whose tendency is to read the Bible in isolation from national or global issues, these Christians have a robust and bold approach to their faith. Eighty thousand of such communities exist in Brazil alone; three hundred operate in Italy. Each has its own character and force. To meet them, share in their liturgy, hear their dialogue sermons is an unforgettable experience.[7]

These grassroots communities are real lights for me, signs of hope in our present world. The background to the Italian groups is as follows. They came into being in Italy after a national congress in 1971 with the definite aim of making the 'class choice' of the poor 'for the renewal of all society'. They did not wish to become a 'super church', nor an up-dated 'with it' branch of the established Roman church, but they saw themselves as a stimulus, a ferment, a sign and witness of a particular message – the Christian one. They went outside and beyond sectarian institutions and dogmatic schemes. If there was to be a characteristic of their entire movement it would flow out of the following: 'In the last twenty years there has been a progressive change in the attitude of many Catholics who have become more and more profoundly conscious of being (the) Church, God's people; this awareness was reflected in Vatican II.' From this 'new awareness' of what it meant to be the people of God came what can only be described, in contemporary Italy at least, as a revolution: 'the people of God, no longer the hierarchy, are the conscious centre of the ecclesia'. There is a total absence of the pietism and unhealthy introversion which Clifford Longley claims is a characteristic of those house churches he describes in the *Times* article. On the contrary, there is a deep political commitment which is fused to their virile form of Christianity and so described: 'these are united by a common deepening of the faith and by a rigorous theological searching based generally on the communitarian reading of the Bible.' They are not withdrawn from the world of ordinary men and women as some sort of pietistic elite, but are all socially active 'carrying out their social-political (and specifically party) engagement in the appropriate secular organization'. One fundamental driving force inspires and unites them: the desire for liberation.

'In the contemporary world, all the renewal paths of society ... and hence also of the Church have their fundamental historic roots in the process of emancipation and liberation of the popular masses which has emerged since the end of the last World War. Centuries old cultural schemes have been called into question *in order to give room for hope* (my italics) for the affirmation of new needs and rights. It is not only a question of the access to consumer goods and a higher standard of living, but also, and above all else, the need of the masses to take their destiny into their own hands and become conscious of themselves as the creators of history and its protagonists.'

Christians are no longer to be treated as children, to be protected from falsehood and error by those who know better, to be spoken down to, or brow-beaten and manipulated by their ecclesiastical superiors who wield inordinate power over them from above. They are to be treated as adults, men and women come of age, capable of dialogue, decision-making, able to exercise mature judgment when offered the facts and allowed to participate in their own destinies. The idea that 'Peter has spoken' is no longer an option for 'Christianity come of age'. When we became adults we put away childish things (I Cor. 13.11) and if this is how God wants the people of God to react, then the people of God should be treated accordingly: 'Brothers you are not to be childish in your outlook. You can be babies as far as wickedness is concerned, but mentally you must be adult' (I Cor. 14.20). This is the breaking process the grassroots Christians in Italy have been engaged in: fighting for the right for people to be allowed to vote as adults, free from the coercion of a right-wing curia; struggling for the right of married couples to decide as responsible adults on such matters as family planning. Above all they have attempted to stand by the poor – the workers, the unemployed, students with a vision for a new world. They have suffered; they have been persecuted by the church's hierarchy, but their vision remains unclouded. They yearn to see a church divested of glorious robes, of massive wealth and humbled to know and serve the poor without condescension. 'The desire and the need to reappropriate the varying dimensions of the life of the church comes from the growth of the human person as subject of history and as a centre which decides freely his/her own life in relationship to other persons along the way. Naturally these relationships vary in depth and degree of common engagement, *but the basis is always equality*' (my italics). For want of a better word this has entailed a 'take over', a reappropriation of the

109

gospel by the poor and on behalf of the poor. They express this process as follows: 'Reappropriation, in itself, is a very meaningful term. Historically it takes the form as reappropriation of the Word of God, of the ministries as true roles of *service*, and of the expressive forms of faith and communitarian life, that is the sacraments. Re-appropriation also means the capacity and possibility to decide autonomously one's position on faith – politics and church – civil society.'

In Italy, with the massive power of the church used to sway political decisions, the importance of such a freedom is of vital importance if a Christian society is to be allowed to come of age and to exercise its democratic rights in a free manner. But the 'reappropriation of the Word of God' by the people is something which would benefit most congregations in England when done within the political and social climate that exists here. The secular must penetrate the church and Christians must be made to face honestly the massive problems of our age as they wrestle with God's word and with their fellow men and women to achieve his liberative justice. We need each other's insights and experiences to help us as we struggle to discover his will for this age. If there are tensions ahead there will also be compensations. 'Another essential and extremely qualifying manner of being the church is the living and sharing of a profoundly felt faith, seen as a tension toward and not as a once and forever patrimony; faith is lived as a contribution to the growth of all ...'[8]

In the achieving of such a church the grassroots communities have suffered a good deal. One abbot of a great Roman church has been deposed; many priests who called for reforms in the Vatican have been compulsorily laicized. They have accepted such violent actions against them with commendable patience, but they have not stopped their struggle. They still meet with congregations which are vigorous, alive and extemely active. The breaking process has been undergone by them, but yet the witness remains. They have emerged from a dry, sterile clericalism and have replaced it with a loving, caring human face in which their fellow Christians share in a total ministry devoid of any form of condescension or religious posturing. Are we to term them religious dissidents, spiritual provocateurs, or the vanguard of a new creation? – I hail them as the latter!

The alienation of our society is something that most priests find extremely threatening and yet we live in a society where we meet it

110

head on. A priest working with a diocesan board for social responsibility told me of a holiday spent as chaplain to a holiday camp. 'I had the unique opportunity on a Saturday night of addressing 6,000 people in the camp theatre,' he told me. 'I told them what the church was about and gave the times of services next day. Seven came to the 8 o'clock communion, a dozen to the family service.'

In Spain the church has got to begin all over again as far as the workers are concerned after its pro-Franco stand during the long reign of the Caudillo. In Madrid I witnessed a revolutionary priest at work. His 'church' was the undercroft of a garage – ordinary workers would not be seen dead in a church. The congregation of about eighty was drawn from the older workers, students and poor people. The walls were whitewashed and near to the reserved sacrament was a small flickering lamp, the only light, next to which was printed in large letters in a script similar to that found in the catacombs the words, 'The Master is here and is waiting for you.' I felt that this underground church had many of the characteristics of the first-century Christians. The priest, dressed like a worker, was called by his Christian name and was absorbed into the community as the eucharist was celebrated. He did not dominate so much as guide it. The youth introduced the theme of the service, and accompanied it with modern hymns, which they had previously practised for about one hour. The people discussed Jesus casting out a devil. They were asked who the modern devils were and one replied, 'The multinationals'. One old lady, who could easily have been transported from the East End of London asked, 'Who are the devils in your country, Colin?' I replied, 'The upholders of apartheid'. The readings were done from simply printed service sheets. Everything was explained before it was attempted. Two wooden chairs were placed at each side of the altar, which was just a simple table. The people faced the priest on three sides. At the prayer of consecration he draped a chasuble over his clothes, took the bread and wine and offered it to God with the people. I do not have words to describe the simplicity, the feeling of togetherness, the sharing, the love. God's poor were my teachers: I was proud to be a part of their worship. I wrote the following some time after as a tribute to a peasant farmer who had participated in the shared sermon. I call it *A Spanish Credo*.

A SPANISH CREDO

You priests
say you know,
but you do not know
what resurrection
really means.

Look
at me: I'm poor,
a peasant, with
stumps for hands,
a back wide as
any barn door,
and legs made for
wrestling with the
stubborn earth.

I know
what resurrection
means, for each
repeating year
I take this seed,
this tiny thing,
and, in the lashing
rain of winter,
kneel on the bare
earth, its grave,
and with uncovered
head bowed in
reverence to my
God cry out,

'Father,
into your hands
I commend this
tiny speck.
Receive it and
breathe the life of
your love upon
it, that when the
spring comes it
will leap up,
as did your
Son, the Lord
Christ, my brother,
that I may harvest
heaven's reward,
the living bread,
which now comes
down to me from
heaven without which
I starve.

This is my credo,
Lord, this tiny
speck of seed
by which you show to me
your power made
perfect in the weakness
of my human need.'

I confess a deep abiding love for these people. They are my friends and my liberators, for they show me that God reigns, that his love shines out in shanties, in prisons and in dank hovels and that darkness does not overcome it. He has allowed me to see him bleeding, broken, despised and rejected, but undeterred and unconquered in the faces of the struggling, hope-filled poor.

Notes

Chapter 1

1. Gustavo Gutierrez, 'The Poor in the Church', quoted in *Towards a Church of the Poor*, edited by Julio de Santa Ana, WCC 1979, p. 122.
2. Ibid., pp. 124f.
3. Julio de Santa Ana, *Towards a Church of the Poor*, WCC 1979, pp. 208f.

Chapter 2

1. Derrick Knight, *Beyond the Pale*, Kogan Page 1980.
2. Defence Force Spokesman, (South Africa) *Sunday Times*, 7 May 1978.
3. James H. Cone, *God of the Oppressed*, SPCK 1977, ·p. 1.
4. Ibid., p. 34.
5. Ibid., p. 55.
6. Ibid., p. 235.
7. Ibid., p. 246.
8. Frei Betto, quoted by Juan Luis Segundo in *The Liberation of Theology*, Gill and Macmillan 1977, p. 239.
9. ·Cone, op. cit., p. 236.
10. Julia Esquivel Velasquez, Correspondence, *International Review of Mission*, WCC July 1977, p. 250.
11. Camilo Torres, quoted by José Míguez Bonino in *Revolutionary Theology Comes of Age*, SPCK 1975, p. 43.
12. Ernesto Cardenal, 'Letter on the Destruction of Solentiname', *NTC News*, Italian Ecumenical News Agency, 10 February 1978, p. 2.

115

13. Milan Machovec, *A Marxist Looks at Jesus*, Darton, Longman and Todd 1976, p.193.

14. Ibid., p.194 (quoting Karl Marx, leading article in *Kölnische Zeitung*, No.179, given in *On Religion*, Foreign Language Publishing House, Moscow, p.35.

15. Ibid., p.202.

16. Ibid., p.204.

Chapter 3

1. *Evangelio, politica y socialismo*, 27 May 1971, Chile.

2. Anglican Church of Namibia, *The Maseru Declaration*, Lesotho 1978, available from the Namibia Peace Centre, 46 Cephas Street, London E1.

Chapter 4

1. James Cone, quoted by Juan Luis Segundo, *The Liberation of Theology*, Gill and Macmillan 1977, p.31.

2. Canaan Banana, 'The Biblical Basis for Liberation Struggles', *International Review of Mission*, WCC October 1979, pp.417-423.

3. Robert Gabriel Mugabe, *Independence Message*, Press Statement, Department of Information, PO Box 8150, Causeway, Salisbury, Zimbabwe, 17 April 1980.

4. Canaan Banana, art. cit., p.423.

5. For the ideas behind these thoughts see Leonardo Boff, *Way of the Cross — Way of Justice*, Orbis Books, Maryknoll 1980.

7. Peter Townsend, *Poverty in the United Kingdom*, Penguin 1979.

8. Karl Marx, *Communist Manifesto*, Penguin ed. 1967, p.80.

9. *The Sunday Times*, 13 July 1980.

10. Fr. Alipio de Freitas, 'Letter to Cardinal Barros Camara, 1964', contained in Alain Gheerbrant, *The Rebel Church in Latin America*, Penguin 1974, pp.328-331.

11. Helder Camara, *Race Against Time*, Sheed and Ward 1971, p.15. (Closing speech to the 6th International Annual Conference of the Catholic Inter-American Cooperation Programme, New York, January 1969).

116

Chapter 5

1. Martin Luther King, *Where Do We Go from Here: Chaos or Community?*, Beacon Press, Boston 1967, p.173; published 1968 by Hodder as *Chaos or Community?*

2. Salary paid to a Secretary in the Church Commissioners.

3. John Downing, *Now you do know*, WOW Campaigns Ltd 1980.

4. Leonardo Boff, *Way of the Cross — Way of Justice*, Orbis Books, Maryknoll 1980, p.99.

5. *Churches Responding to Racism in the 1980s* (Working Papers for the WCC Consultation, The Netherlands, June 1980), WCC PCR Report Paper No.6, p.65.

6. Letter from Coordinadora Nacional de la Iglesia Popular 'Oscar a Romero' (CONIP), El Salvador, 8 August 1980, to the comrades of the Committees of Solidarity with the people of El Salvador, at their regional conference.

7. Letter from Archbishop Romero to President Jimmy Carter, translated from a French version brought to the Namibia Peace Centre by two doctors from El Salvador.

Chapter 6

1. Justin Martyr, from *The First Apology*.

2. William Temple, *Readings in St John's Gospel*, Macmillan 1945; 1961 ed., pp.275f.

3. Thomas Merton, *Conjectures of a Guilty Bystander*, Burns & Oates 1968, pp.140ff.; reissued Sheldon Press 1977.

4. Leonardo Boff, *Jesus Christ Liberator*, Orbis Books, Maryknoll 1978, p.220.

5. Lisandero de la Torre, 'The Generation of the '30s', quoted in Ernesto Cardenal, *Cuba*, New Directions Publishing Corporation, NY 1974, pp.161f.

6. *The Times*, 11 August 1980.

7. See Ernesto Cardenal, *Love in Practice: The Gospel in Solentiname*, Search Press 1977.

8. See *Specific Characteristics of the Italian Christian Grassroots Communities*, NTC News, (Italian Ecumenical News Agency), June Special 1980.